STORIES
for the
Spirit-
filled™
Believer

STORIES
for the
Spirit-filled ™
Believer

Edited by Cristine Bolley

STARBURST PUBLISHERS™

P.O. Box 4123, Lancaster, PA 17604
www.starburstpublishers.com

To schedule author appearances,
write: Author Appearances,
Starburst Promotions,
P. O. Box 4123, Lancaster,
PA 17604 or call (717) 293-0939.
Website: www.starburstpublishers.com

CREDITS:
Cover design by Richmond & Williams
Text design and composition by Booksetters

Unless otherwise indicated all Scripture is taken from the Holy Bible:
New International Version® NIV®. Copyright 1973, 1978, 1984 by
International Bible Society. Used by permission of Zondervan
Publishing House.

Other Bible versions used are indicated by the following abbreviations:
The Amplified Bible (AMP)
The Living Bible (TLB)
New American Standard Bible (NASB)
New King James Version (NKJV)
King James Version (KJV)

STORIES FOR THE SPIRIT-FILLED BELIEVER
Copyright © 2001 by Starburst Publishers, Inc.
All rights reserved.

First Printing, November 2001

ISBN 1-892016-54-0
Library of Congress Card Number: 2001088301
Printed in the United States of America

Contents

❧ He Restores Our Souls ❧

❧ We Will Fear No Evil ❧

❧ He Anoints Us ❧

∽ Goodness and Mercy Follows Us ∿

The Lord Is My Shepherd

An early desire to be led by the Spirit was ignited in me when I read *The Cross and the Switchblade* by David Wilkerson. His testimony of how God asked him to preach the gospel in New York City and the subsequent revival of gang member Nicky Cruz stirred a longing in me for an intimate relationship with God.

A few weeks later, I begged God for His presence in my life as I walked home from church in the pouring rain. Salty tears burst forth from the flooded reservoir in my heart, and pure water from the thunderous clouds above washed them away as I cried out, *"Lord, I want to hear Your voice. I want to know that I am a part of something bigger than myself, something that proves we are each an important piece of some worthwhile destiny."*

Within weeks of that prayer, a teenage boy named Mark, a stranger to me, knocked on my door and said, "I have been in prayer and God sent me to tell you that you are to go to Mexico to work for Him, but before you go, you need to be baptized with the power and fire of the Holy Spirit."

I remember saying to Mark, "Well, I'll believe it when I see it in His Word."

A few days later, I read Paul's question to the disciples in Ephesus (Acts 19:1–6), "Did you receive the Holy Spirit when you believed on Jesus as the Christ?" Those believers answered, "No, we have not even heard that there is a Holy Spirit." On hearing Paul's testimony, they were baptized again, this time in the name of the Lord Jesus. As Paul laid his hands on them, the Holy Spirit came upon them and they spoke in new languages and prophesied.

I had loved the Father God since I was four and was saved through faith in Jesus when I was twelve, but I had never even heard of fellowship with the Holy Spirit that is spoken of in 2 Corinthians 13:14. The Holy Spirit had been *with* me, and *in* me, but I had not yet experienced the coming *upon* of His power to witness. I finally asked Mark to pray with me to receive all God had for me.

I sensed that powers in both heaven and hell witnessed my commitment to the Lord that day. A new word came to my mind after praying, but I was hesitant to speak it out. I had never heard or read it before; it was *Abba*. When Mark heard me whisper the word, he asked, "Don't you know what that word means? It is the Greek word for Father. It's the name that Jesus called to in the garden of Gethsemane."

He showed me where the word was written in Mark 14:36; Romans 8:15; and Galatians 4:6 which reads, "Because you are sons, God sent the Spirit of his Son into our hearts, the Spirit who calls out, "Abba, Father." The written Word confirmed my experience.

With one word from the Father, I became intimately aware of His power to resolve the destiny of my life. The Scriptures seemed suddenly clear to me as if someone had given me the glasses needed for a 3-D movie.

By the time I was eighteen, I was on my way to a mission in Mexico where I worked for a year with other missionaries to build churches for new believers—just as Mark had prophesied to me a few months before. I learned to be totally dependent on God; I learned that the Lord is my Shepherd and I did not lack. Now, over thirty years later I have learned that the Lord is faithful to keep those who have been given to Him.

I have also learned that spiritual gifts are given to demonstrate God's love to individuals who need His grace and mercy. If we want to see God's miracles, we must go to where the people are who have needs and believe God will meet those needs as these stories illustrate.

The stories in this book testify of the Lord's ability and desire to save and rescue us; He refreshes and restores us; He leads us in the way we should go; and He blesses us with goodness, mercy and unfailing love just as Psalm 23 promises.

Jesus said, "My sheep hear my voice, and I know them, and they follow me" (John 10:27 KJV). The authors in this book come from diverse cultures, unique callings, and varied emphases of ministry yet they share a place in the Shepherd's flock and enjoy the peace that comes from responding to His voice. They know the Shepherd because they abide in Him.

Bruce Wilkerson writes in *The Secret of the Vine,* "Abiding begins with visible spiritual disciplines, such as Bible reading and prayer. Yet it may shock you to find out that *we can do these things for years without abiding.* After all, reading a book about a person isn't the same thing as knowing the person who wrote the book. The challenge in abiding is always to break through from dutiful activities to a living, flourishing relationship with God."

All the stories you will read in this book are from people who flourish in such a relationship with God. They hear His voice and their obedience makes them aware of God's presence every day. If you have never heard the voice of God before, it is my hope and the intent of my publisher that the testimonies in this book will inspire you to listen for His daily Word for you.

The prayers included at the end of the stories are paraphrased scriptures to release His perfect will and gifts in us so that we will reveal His goodness to others. An asterisk (*) following a name indicates that it has been changed.

May these stories reignite your passion to listen for the voice of God and respond to His invitation to carry the Shepherd's message of love to someone in need of His compassion.

HE RESCUES US

The Lord is my Shepherd [to feed, guide, and shield me], I shall not lack.

—Psalm 23:1 AMP

It is fun to follow Jesus as our Shepherd because we feel safe when we follow His voice. He feeds us, increasing our faith, and guides us to help others and protects us from danger. My first assignment from the Shepherd led me to a *green* house on a street called *Lime* and eventually to "a lost lamb" named Pam *Green*. Each piece of the puzzle built my faith along the way.

Beth Moore's encounter with the wild-haired man creates a godly desire in all of us to be sensitive to the Lord's instruction. Riveting accounts of rescue from fire, plane crashes, and head-on collisions included in these pages will give reason to be thankful we have a Shepherd Who knows what is around the next curve in the road of life.

The story "The Night Vision," by Ruth Offutt, confirms that God will not abandon us, and the story from Jesse Duplantis proves that the Shepherd is our ever-present shield of protection.

Lead the Way, Lord

By Cristine Bolley

When I was eighteen, I was invited to a thriving church in the heart of Kansas City. I don't remember who the speaker was that night, but I clearly remember his exhortation, "Ask God to give you an assignment. Then be still and wait until you hear His voice."

I closed my eyes and prayed, *"Lord, lead me to someone You want to reach, or to something I can do to be involved in Your work."*

Conversational words quickly poured into my thoughts, saying, *"I want you to give away some of your clothes."*

7

"OK, *where shall I take them?*" I asked (not out loud, but in my spirit).

"*To 12th and Lime,*" responded the Voice.

"*When should I go?*"

"*Monday, at 1:30 P.M., and not before.*"

"*How will I know which house to go to?*"

"*It will be a green house.*"

A *green* house at 12th and *Lime*? Who would paint their house green? And what are the odds that a green house will be on a street called Lime! It was crazier than any fiction I could have dreamed up.

Early Monday morning, I went to my closet and began sorting clothes to give away. *"This one, Lord?"* I asked with each item. Sometimes I heard *"no,"* and sometimes *"yes,"* and sometimes I asked twice to be sure He had said yes to one of my favorite outfits. Before long, I had a big pile of clothes lying on my bed ready to take to my car.

> *I asked twice to be sure when God said yes to my favorite outfits.*

I knew there was a street called Lime in South Topeka, but I also knew it became a dead end at a greenbelt before getting to 12th Street. I didn't know whether or not it continued on the north side of the woods. Eager to see if the corner even existed, I carried the clothes out to my car and thought I would just check out the neighborhood. But I felt a strong impression within me that I wasn't to leave yet, so I returned to the house and sat down in the living room. My eyes grew heavy, and though it was only 11:00 A.M., I fell into a deep sleep until I was startled awake at 1:15 P.M.—just enough time to get to my assignment.

I had never been in the northeast part of town and didn't know my way through this neighborhood. I had to weave through various side streets; yet, it was exactly 1:30 P.M. when I turned east on 12th Street and saw the street sign for Lime. I was surprised to find this intersection, but I was even more amazed to find that three families at the corner of 12th and Lime had painted their houses bright, lime green!

A sense of reverence filled me as I realized God was indeed directing my steps. No one was home at the first two houses. When a woman finally answered the door of the third house, I could see she was struggling to hold back two dogs including a large German shepherd that wasn't happy to see me. She asked what I wanted through the two-inch opening of her door.

"Is anyone here about my size who could use some clothes?" I asked.

There was an awkward pause. Then the woman answered, "Give them to the Lord, honey, and He will give you your reward."

"But I did give them to God and He told me to come here!"

"Wait while I put the dogs away," she said. A few minutes later the woman invited me to come in. We talked for nearly an hour. Suddenly she said, "I will pray for you now." She laid her hands upon my shoulders and said, "Lord, direct this child to the person that You have meant to receive these clothes. Guide her steering wheel in the way she should go."

Dazed, yet still intrigued, I left the corner of 12th and Lime and began looking for a teenage girl, who might want my gift of clothes. Finally, I headed west via the 10th Street bridge, and there I noticed a young girl walking the opposite direction toward the neighborhood I had just left.

"Is that her?" I asked the Lord.

But this time there was no voice. *What have I got to lose by asking her?* I thought as I turned the car around.

There was no traffic, so I rolled down the window on the passenger's side and asked if she wanted a ride. She looked a little frightened, shook her head no, and said, "Sure." As soon as she got into the car, she said, "I never accept rides from strangers! I don't even know why I got in!"

"This ride is from the Lord," I explained. "I have clothes in my backseat to give away, and He told me to come here. Would you be able to use any of those outfits?"

She glanced at the pile and said, "Well, I have a lot of cousins who might use them if they don't fit me." Then she looked at me carefully and asked, "So are you an angel?"

I laughed and told her where I had been born, where I lived, and how the minister in Kansas City told me to ask God for an assignment. Her house was only a few blocks from the bridge. She invited me in and I helped carry the clothes to her room. She told me her mother had wanted her to go to church and that maybe she would go after all.

"By the way," I asked as I was leaving, "My name is Cris, what's yours?"

"Pam Green," she answered.

Green!—as in green *houses at 12th and* Lime? Had God gone to so much trouble to plant clues in green houses on a street named for the color green, to send me to someone for prayer, and to cause delays so that I would know I had found the right person, Pam Green, just as she was crossing the bridge? She, too, was surprised as I recounted the "coincidences" that led me to finding her. "God really loves you, Pam!" I told her.

About a week later, I stopped to see her and she greeted me with a brilliant smile. "Guess what?" she said. "I went to church with my mom the night after you came and I gave my life to the Lord! I'm getting baptized next week. Are you sure you're not an angel?" she asked half teasing, yet looking for a halo.

> Then the master told his servant, "Go out to the roads and country lanes and make them come in, so that my house will be full."
>
> —Luke 14:23

Lord,

Guide me in Your truth and faithfulness and teach me, for You are the God of my salvation; for You [You only and altogether] do I wait expectantly all day long.

Amen

May I Have the Pleasure?

By Beth Moore

I was heading to the East Coast and I had a layover in Knoxville. Because I was changing from a large airplane to a small one, I was in a large room with several exits to airplanes out each door. The room was filled with people waiting to get on the smaller planes.

I had about an hour to wait and was sitting with my Bible on my lap, trying to memorize John chapter 1. I had worked on memorizing it before and had found that the best way to memorize is to read something out loud and then stare out the window and then say it from memory. I got to a place in John 1 where I stumbled and the woman next to me filled in the line. I realized that she had heard it so many times that she was memorizing it as well.

I had had a marvelous morning with the Lord. I had the book on my lap and was very intent on what I was doing when I noticed the people that were sitting in front of me. I saw that their attention suddenly had gone over my shoulder and they were staring at something, and I could tell from their expressions it was something horrifying.

What in the world is going on behind me? I thought. I wanted to look so badly, but I didn't want to be obvious. I had to wait for that proper moment, not when everyone else was looking, but for *my* chance to look. So I was still trying to stare at my Bible, but I was checking them out, thinking, *Whatever's going on . . . it's a good one.*

In just a few minutes I could see activity over my left shoulder. Finally, I glanced over my shoulder out the corner of my eye. I saw a sight I will never forget.

It was an airline hostess pushing a wheelchair with an old man that looked like he could not be less than 127 years old. I have never seen a human being look that old and that weary and that drawn. I tried to keep from staring, but he was such a strange figure. He was humped over in the wheelchair. He was the skinniest man I had ever seen and his knees were protruding from his trousers. His shoulders looked like he still had his coat hanger in his shirt. His hands were veins and bones. But the strangest part of it was that his gray hair was about to the middle of his back. His fingernails were at least as long as mine—not painted, thank goodness, but they were long.

I put down my Bible and thought, *I wonder what's wrong with that man?* I was trying to read the Word to keep from seeing what God was trying to show me. I was staring down at that book because I'd rather be preoccupied right here than to touch it out there! I was looking down at the Bible and my heart was overwhelmed. I already knew and was beginning to resist because I could feel God pulling on my spirit and working on my heart. I was being moved toward that man.

I could feel God pulling my spirit and moving me toward that man.

I thought, *"Oh no, God. Please no."* I began to argue with God in my mind. I was thinking to myself and looking up at God. *"Please, I know what's going on here. You want me to witness to this man, don't You? God, please don't make me witness to this man. Please, I'll do anything. Put me on the same plane as him. I'll witness to him there, but don't make me get up here and go witness to this man."*

I don't have a problem witnessing—sharing the gospel with someone. I love doing that. But he was a peculiar-looking man and everyone was *looking* at the peculiar-looking man. As I was staring down, trying to keep my concentration on the Word and trying to have this argument with God, I felt Him move upon my heart. When I say God spoke to me, it wasn't audible—it was in my heart. I always know it's God if it's consistent with His Word, I'm in the spirit, and it's out in left field. I'm still thinking, *"God, please don't make me witness to this man. Not now! I'll do it on the plane, if You'll put us on the same plane."*

God spoke as clearly in my spirit as I would talk to you. *"I don't want you to witness to him. I want you to brush his hair."*

I dropped my chin, looked back up at God, and said, *"I want You to know I am ready to witness to this man. I am on this man, Lord! You have never seen a woman witness to a* man faster. *What difference does it make if his hair is a mess or not if he is not redeemed? I'm on this man."*

"*That's not what I said, Beth. I do not want you to witness to him. I want you to go brush his hair.*"

I looked up at God and thought, *Well, I don't have a hairbrush.* I mean, I spray my hair and that's it!

But as I started walking, I could hear Him saying, "*I will thoroughly furnish you in all your works.*"

I walked up to the man and knelt in front of him and I whispered, "Sir . . . may I have the pleasure of brushing your hair?"

He looked back up at me and said, "What'd you say?"

"May I have the pleasure of brushing your hair?" I spoke a little louder.

He said, "Little lady, if you want me to hear you, you're gonna have to speak a little louder than that."

So I said, "Sir, MAY I HAVE THE PLEASURE OF BRUSHING YOUR HAIR?" At this point every eye in the airport turned straight into my face. I could feel my face turn crimson; it was burning.

He looked up at me with absolute shock and said, "If you really want to."

I thought, *No, I don't want to . . . I don't want to,* but I replied, "Yes, sir. I would be so pleased, but I have one little problem. I don't have a hairbrush."

He said, "I have one in my bag."

I went around to the back of that wheelchair and I got down on my hands and knees, and began lifting out undershirts and pajamas. I finally came to the bottom of the bag and found the hairbrush. I stood up and started brushing his hair. It was clean, but it was tangled into mats. But I had experience and I began brushing at the bottom.

A miraculous thing happened to me as I started brushing his hair. Everybody else in that place disappeared. There was no one alive for those moments except that old man and me. I brushed and brushed until every tangle was out of his hair. I walked around him and put my hands on his knees and got down on my knees in front of him. I said, "Sir, do you know Jesus?"

He said, "Yes, I do. That figures . . . that figures. I've known him since I married my bride. She wouldn't marry me until I got to know the Savior. See the problem is I haven't seen my bride in months. I've had open-heart surgery, and she's been too ill to come see me. I was sitting here thinking to myself 'What a mess I must be for my bride.'"

> *God knows your need. He sees you.*

I'll never forget it. Soon the airline hostess came to get him and we said our good-byes. Sadly, we were not on the same plane and I wish we had been. I was very ashamed of how I had acted. The stewardess rolled him onto that plane, and I still had a few minutes to wait. When she came out, tears were streaming down her cheeks.

She said, "That old man sitting in the plane is sobbing. Why did you do that? What made you do that?"

I said, "Do you know Jesus? He's the bossiest thing!" I was able to share the gospel with her.

I learned something that day that I will never forget. He knows if you're exhausted, if you're hungry, if you're serving in the wrong place, if it's time to move on, or if you just need your hair brushed. God knows your need. He sees *you* as an individual. Tell Him your need.

> Then you will call, and the LORD will answer; you will cry for help, and he will say: Here am I. "If you do

away with the yoke of oppression, with the pointing finger and malicious talk, and if you spend yourselves in behalf of the hungry and satisfy the needs of the oppressed, then your light will rise in the darkness, and your night will become like the noonday."

—Isaiah 58:9–10

Lord,

You are good, a refuge in times of trouble.
You care for those who trust in You.

Amen

Obedience— the Cutting Edge

By Elizabeth Wietholter

As a young married couple, my husband and I were stationed by the U.S. Air Force at Fort Lewis, Washington—my husband's first duty assignment after college ROTC. The time in Washington turned out to be a spiritual hotbed for us. Separated from our roots and traditions, we were open to the Spirit of God and He led us in new paths. Daily He taught us what it meant to be disciples of Jesus.

One of our great joys was the beauty of nature around our new home. Mountains, rain forest, ocean, islands beckoned to us and were an easy day trip, just a few hours from home. Nearly every week we'd drive to some mountain or forest, take photos, and drink in the wonders created by the awesome God we were coming to know better and better.

One day we piled our gear into our Pinto station wagon and set out on a three-hour drive to the Washington coastline to see the ocean for the first time. We've always enjoyed driving together and, as usual, had one of our best conversations in the relaxed atmosphere of the car that day, sharing our hearts and thoughts.

Suddenly, Ray said, "I'll drive!"

I was taking my turn at the wheel as we traveled on a two-lane road through a Pacific forest about an hour from our destination. Suddenly, Ray said, "Why don't you pull over and I'll drive?"

"Oh, I'm doing fine," I replied. "I really haven't been driving that long."

About a mile later, he said again, somewhat more insistently, "Pull over here and I'll take over at the wheel."

"No, really!" I repeated. "I'm doing fine. I'm enjoying driving right now."

Ten seconds later, his strong voice, tinged with anger, boomed from the passenger seat, "I said, pull over so I can drive. Pull over here. Now."

As I considered whether to continue in my own stubborn way or to comply with Ray's words, a memory flashed into my mind of a discipleship principle I had been studying—"Wives, submit to your husbands as to the Lord" (Ephesians 5:22).

I had a decision to make and I knew it. My feelings of pride resisted obeying my husband, but the witness of the Spirit within me was clear. With feelings hurt and "feathers ruffled," I applied the brake, pulled to the side of the road, threw the gearshift into park, and jumped out of the driver's door in a huff to walk around the car and exchange seats with my husband.

As I rounded the trunk heading for the passenger door, a spine-chilling roar pulled my eyes back to the roadway. On the curve just ahead of us, two huge logging trucks, fully loaded with tons of enormous tree trunks, roared side-by-side around the curved and narrow two-lane road.

Had we gone a few seconds more, we would have been killed.

There was no shoulder around that curve, and large trees grew right along the roadside. Immediately, the realization hit us that had we gone on even a few more seconds, our car would have hit those trucks head-on! Only because of Ray's insistence, I had pulled off at the last possible place to escape being smashed to smithereens.

Ray and I both lived that day, contrary to the enemy's plan to destroy us, because of our simple acts of obedience. Ray obeyed by speaking up. I obeyed by yielding to his direction. Both of us learned eternal lessons through that experience—the importance of boldness in leadership, the protection of headship, and the power of simple obedience to the voice of the Holy Spirit through divinely established authority.

God's directions to us are always more important than our feelings and opinions, and pride is always a tool of the enemy to detour us from the way of blessing.

Submit to every human authority for the Lord's sake.

—1 Peter 2:13

Lord,

You are my shield who saves the upright in heart.

Amen

The Christmas Miracle

By Victoria Craig

I will never forget Christmas day when my son, Nelson, was sixteen months old. We lived in Houston in a house so old it had a floor register for heat in the dining room. It was cold for Houston that year, and because I had the heater on I had to watch that my children didn't get burned on the grid.

We were supposed to be all snuggled in our beds, but at two in the morning I sat straight up in bed with fear telling me something was terribly wrong.

I rushed to the children's bedroom. The girls were there, but Nelson was missing.

I hurried back into the short hall. As I stood there, I noticed the door to the dining room was closed. I had left it open so we could keep warm. I ran over, pulled the door open, and spotted my son in a blanket "nest" on the floor register. Nelson was asleep on top of my coat, his oldest sister's coat, and his favorite blanket.

Just as I saw him, the blankets burst into flames.

I ran the few steps to him, picked him up with my right hand, and picked up the burning material with my left hand. I tossed the bundle of flames against the wall. Thankfully, the fire went out.

I saw my son just as the coats and blanket burst into flames.

I looked to see if my still-sleeping son was burned. He wasn't, so I took him to bed. As I covered him up, I realized my left hand hurt. I looked at both of my hands. My right hand and my son were not burned. But my left palm and fingers were severely burned, except for a small place on the base of my hand. Blisters were already forming. I ran to the kitchen and got a rag and some ice. I stayed up and held the ice and cried the rest of the night.

The next morning I got the children ready to go to my parent's home for Christmas. I held ice and got three toddlers ready with one hand and much fidgeting.

Christmas at my parents' home was a wondrous thing because we celebrated the Twelve Days of Christmas with various friends who reminded us when it was their day to rejoice with us. Christmas Day we had the most guests, and that year there were thirty of us. I normally helped with the cooking, but that day I held ice and watched the babies. My sister, Kathie, made sure I had enough ice.

Just before it was time to eat, my father invited those who wanted to pray for my hand to gather around me. Four preachers, friends, and family gathered around me as my father anointed me and said, "Victoria has always had a great faith in healing. She needs healing for her hand. Let's pray."

They reached out and touched me or the person standing between them and me. My father prayed aloud as the others prayed silently in agreement. It was a wonder-filled moment.

After they finished praying, I looked at my hand. It looked as if it had never been burned.

There were two miracles that day: God warned me to save my son from the midst of burning coats, and God healed my hand. To this day I remind my son of the miracle and tell him God saved him for a reason. And I remind myself that God loves me, and He has shown me His miracles. So if anyone tries to tell you that the age of miracles is past, you might tell them, "Miracles have passed away only for those who don't believe."

> Believe me when I say that I am in the Father and the Father is in me; or at least believe on the evidence of the miracles themselves.
>
> —John 14:11

Lord,

You give us Your Spirit and work miracles among us because we believe what we have heard. Thank you for crediting us as righteous because we believe in You.

Amen

The Lost Lamb

By Suzy Ryan

"Mom, are you going to comb your hair before my soccer game?" my six-year-old daughter, Lauren, asked as we scrambled to the car.

In the morning rush, I'd barely had enough time to brush my teeth, much less worry about how I looked. Since I hadn't even prayed, I packed my backpack with my Bible and journal. *While Lauren warms up*, I thought, *I'll have some time with God.*

When we arrived at the field, I saw a circus of police cars and a hysterical woman sobbing and flailing her hands in despair. Lauren's coach informed me that an hour before, the same woman had dropped off her son for his game. After she'd parked the car, she couldn't find him. The police searched the complex, but there was no trace of the six-year-old boy.

"*Go pray with her*," God seemed to say to my heart.

"*No way!*" I answered God in my mind. "*How can I impose on her in her greatest hour of need? I just can't do it.*"

"*Go pray with her. It'll encourage her,*" God said again.

The nudging in my spirit refused to be quenched, and I found myself ambling toward this desperate mother.

"Can I pray with you?" I asked.

"Please, my son Tyler has disappeared," she said.

I hugged her, and she relaxed in my arms. Then I prayed the words from Psalm 91:11, asking God to protect Tyler and perform a miracle by quickly finding him.

I got an overwhelming urge to help look for Tyler.

Suddenly, I had this overwhelming urge to run down the soccer field and look for Tyler myself. Halfway down the field, I crossed the street near a parking lot.

A woman with a van full of children asked me, "Are you looking for a lost little boy?"

My stomach dropped to my toes. "Yes!" I answered.

"I saw a little boy about forty-five minutes ago walking down the street," she said pointing to the four-lane road with cars streaming by us.

"Please, come tell the police," I begged.

The woman told her children to wait, and raced off with me to tell her story to the officers. They showed her a picture of Tyler and she said, "Yes, that's him."

They immediately radioed for reinforcements to search the road for Tyler.

I returned to my daughter's game, but kept my eye on the frantic mother. About fifteen minutes later, I saw the woman beaming and I rushed over to her.

"They found him!" she shouted. "Two miles down the road. He's safe. He's OK."

"I'm so relieved for you!"

"Thank you for your help," she said, her eyes watering. "It was your tip that was the start of finding my Tyler."

"It was God's miracle," I answered. "I didn't even want to come over to you, but I felt Him urging me to pray with you. Jesus loves you and Tyler so much! This was His tender gift to you, and it all started after we prayed. If you don't go to church, I suggest you find one. God has great plans for you and Tyler."

I gave her one last hug and returned to watch the rest of Lauren's game. After the match, my daughter and I skipped to the parking lot thanking God for protecting Tyler.

When I got to the car, I looked back at the field. The Lord's glory still shone around the soccer complex. What an intimate "quiet time" I'd had with Him, and He didn't even care that my hair was a mess. He just wanted me to be available—available to experience His miracle.

> "Because he loves me," says the LORD, "I will rescue him; I will protect him, for he acknowledges my name. He will call upon me, and I will answer him; I will be with him in trouble, I will deliver him and honor him. With long life will I satisfy him and show him my salvation."
>
> —Psalm 91:14–16

Lord,

Thank You for coming to seek and save
those of us who are lost, and for rejoicing
when we are found.

Amen

$\mathcal{A}$ Time

to $\mathcal{P}$ray

BY A. STARR CLAY

My dad, Jim Adkins, has been retired from his career as a captain and chief pilot/instructor for American Airlines for a number of years, but he frequently recalls God's goodness and care for him and those who flew with him. One story, however, is so remarkable that I would not believe it if anyone but my father had told it.

Dad was driving home after a trip one afternoon when he happened to see a former pastor, "Happy" Eliason. Happy waved him in for a visit.

"What happened to you last Saturday afternoon at 3:15?" Happy asked.

"Nothing," Dad said. "I flew but the trip was routine."

Happy explained that he was driving down a quiet rural road toward his home on Saturday afternoon at about 3:15. Suddenly, he literally saw Dad's face on his windshield, and he was overwhelmed by an urgent and persuasive need to stop and pray for Dad. So he did.

At 3:15 P.M. on Saturday he saw Dad's face on the windshield and stopped to pray.

"Well," Dad said, "your prayer was so effective I didn't even know I was in danger."

On the weekend following his visit with Happy, Dad decided to replace an assigned captain since the rest of our family planned to be away. Dad loved to fly, and the all-expense-paid layover at a gorgeous hotel on the beach in Santa Monica, California, was a bonus!

The weather was beautiful everywhere along the route except in the Mississippi River valley. In the valley there was a layer of clouds about 5,000 feet thick starting about 7,000 feet above ground.

Cruising at 18,000 feet, Dad was cleared to descend to 8,000 feet for approach into (a stop in) Memphis. The plane was traveling at about 530 knots as they entered the cloud tops and it became noticeably rougher. His radar showed thinner clouds to his right.

Always alert to his passengers' comfort, he told the first officer to radio the control tower that he would slow down to 250 knots and alter his course 15 degrees right. As the first officer picked up his mike, Dad began a right aileron input, which moved the airfoil on the edge of the plane's wing, enabling a gentle right turn.

Before the first officer could press his mike button, the air traffic controller came on the air. He was screaming, "American 383! Turn 90 degrees right *immediately!*" Not 15 degrees—which would be normal for traffic separation—but 90 degrees!

Since the frantic voice suggested some peril on his left, Dad turned his head to look left. The right turn had raised his left wingtip a few feet—just enough for a DC-9 to slip beneath his wing with inches to spare.

In a momentary break in the clouds, the face Dad saw passing beneath his left wing was the captain of a Southern Airways DC-9 in his cockpit climbing northeast bound for Nashville. Dad learned later that the Southern flight was in an accelerating climb going about 275 knots, while Dad's Boeing 727 was descending, slowing, at about 325 knots. A collision of any proportion would have meant certain death for everyone aboard both planes.

Dad turned to look at the copilot. He, too, had seen the DC-9 and was ashen and goggle-eyed. Once on the ground in Memphis, my shaken father learned that the air traffic controller had forgotten that he had cleared Southern to climb and American to descend, effectively placing both planes in the same airspace.

Later that day as Dad walked down to the beach, he thanked God that he was alive. The setting sun was beautiful, life was good, and he knew he would recognize his dependence on God and His tender, unmerited mercies more in the future.

Then a startling thought occurred to him: The near collision was at 3:15 P.M. on Saturday. God had answered Happy's prayer, which was uttered one week before the event—not just to the day and hour—but, as nearly as he could tell, to the exact minute.

> Because Jesus lives forever, he has a permanent priesthood. Therefore he is able to save completely those who come to God through him, because he always lives to intercede for them.
>
> —Hebrews 7:24–25

Lord,

I will sing praise to Your name, and fulfill my vows to You day after day, for You have appointed Your love and faithfulness to protect me.

Amen

He Took
My
Steering Wheel

By Dr. Anna Rich

It was a hot Saturday morning over twenty years ago. As usual we all were doing our chores. My husband and sons were doing yard work. The boys had cleaned their rooms. I had fixed breakfast and was doing the dishes.

Six weeks before we had buried our beautiful, exuberant, ten-year-old daughter. She had been fatally wounded in a boating accident. Often I cried and I prayed, *"Oh, Lord, no mother should have to endure this horrible pain."* Today was no different. As I swished the dishes through the hot soapy water, I lifted my right hand to my cheek to wipe away the tears.

Suddenly, a sense of urgency was impressed on me and God said, *"Go to the park!"*

Going to the park was not unusual for me, because I went there weekly to speak with people and to give them salvation tracts about Jesus. My friend Mary Louise and I had just printed ten thousand tracts, which we were planning to hand out that summer, but Saturday was chore day. Yet that inner voice urged, *"Go quickly!"*

I dried my hands, grabbed my keys and purse, and walked toward the garage.

"Honey, where are you going?" my husband asked.

"God told me to go to the park!" I yelled. Then I jumped in my van and took off as my husband stared at me with his mouth hanging open.

There are two small parks and a large one near our home in Long Beach. *"Which park, Lord?"* I asked.

No answer.

I drove by the closest park, searching for "something," but what? *"Lord, please, tell me what to do."*

After driving by the other little park, I decided to go home since nothing seemed to be happening. I drove toward our neighborhood and even thought that maybe I was going a lit-tle nutty from the grief over my daughter.

As I tried to turn into the section where we lived, my steer-ing wheel would not turn and I had to keep driving straight ahead. It became clear to me the Lord wanted me to go to Scherer Park. I passed another big intersection and tried again to make a turn, just to test if I was imagining the resistance and to see if it was the Lord Who had kept me from turning before. But again, I could *not* make the turn and had to keep going straight ahead. At the intersection of Atlantic Avenue I was able to finally take a left turn. I found a parking space in the nearly full park-ing lot. It was over 90 degrees that hot summer day.

"Now what, Lord?"

No answer.

I decided to get out of my car and just go around the parking lot and hand out tracts. By now I was thinking that I was wasting my time and should be home doing my chores! After handing out about twenty-five tracts and still having no idea what God wanted me to do, I was feeling hot and miserable. I decided to leave.

But my eyes focused on a car far away in the last space of the parking lot. *Oh, that is too far and I am out of tracts, besides I am only imagining I am needed here,* I reasoned.

When I tried to unlock the car door, the key would not work. I looked up, glanced back at that far-away car, and said, *"OK, I get the hint. I'll check it out."*

> *I could not unlock my car. "OK, God," I said, "I get the hint."*

As I came near the car, my heart started to pound. *What am I getting myself into?* I saw the window on the driver's side was open about six inches. My thoughts raced. *Nobody is in it. Wait, what is that on the backseat? Oh, dear God in heaven—a baby!*

Instinctively I yelled, "Help! Help!" I tore open the door, which was not locked.

I grabbed the baby, a beautifully dressed little girl. Her color was strange, she had drops of perspiration on her forehead and above her lips, she was shaking as though she was having a seizure, and she felt limp and at the same time stiff in my arms.

"Help! Help!" I screamed, my mind still racing, yet my thoughts were clear. *This child is about to die from heat exposure.*

Two people who responded to my cry for help stand out in my memories of that day. One was a large, African American woman whose body moved and shook as she ran toward me. The other was a man with a big belly and a beer in his hand who hollered, "What's going on? What's going on?"

I frantically babbled, telling how I had found the little girl. "I was washing my dishes and God told me to go to the park and I did and I didn't know what He wanted, but I just looked at this car and I found this baby! Oh, Lord, she would have died! Please, help!" I grabbed the man's ice-cold drink and poured some on the baby and held the cold can at the nape of her neck.

> "Help!" I screamed. "This baby is dying!"

The large lady stood near me with her arms folded over her chest, nodding her head and saying, "I believe it, I believe it."

I wanted to hug her. For some reason I felt grateful that she was backing me up in my faith in God. Then—thank God—the baby started to whimper and held on to me for dear life.

"Come. Follow me. Let's find the parents," I said. We must have been quite a sight. I headed up the parade with the beautifully-clad baby girl in my arms. The man with the belly, the wonderful lady—she was not going to miss this—the others who overheard my story, and more followed as we proceeded into the park.

We saw a large crowd at a little waterfall area in the park. A bride and groom were there with their nicely dressed wedding guests. Many turned around to observe our parade.

"Whose baby is this?" I asked.

A sweet, young couple came to me and held out their hands to their baby.

I did not want to let go of her. They did not speak English so I asked for an interpreter. I wanted them to hear my story of how God had told me to come to the park. How I had prayed that no other mother should ever have to endure the loss of a beloved child. I had the interpreter tell them that God had mercy on them and did not allow their baby to die and to never ever leave the baby in the car alone, neither in the heat nor the cold.

Then I handed their baby to them. I looked around and saw that many people were crying. Some people slapped me on the shoulder to show their support and approval; some hugged me. I felt shaky.

As I walked back to my van, I had mixed emotions. Here I was, saving a baby's life after so recently losing my own daughter. As I drove home, I felt both sad and glad, satisfied and accomplished—like a hero.

God had heard my prayer and instantly answered me by sending me on assignment to save a life and spare a family from tragedy. Psalm 37:23 tells us, "The steps of the righteous are ordered by the Lord!" I thanked the Lord for ordering my steps to save this child.

> For you make me glad by your deeds, O Lord; I sing for joy at the works of your hands. How great are your works, O Lord, how profound are your thoughts!
>
> —Psalm 92:4–5

Lord,

I delight greatly in You; my soul rejoices in You, my God. For You have clothed me with garments of salvation and arrayed me in a robe of righteousness.

Amen

The Night Vision

By Ruth Woodbury-Craig Offutt

"For God does speak—now one way, now another—though man may not perceive it. In a dream, in a vision of the night, when deep sleep falls on men as they slumber in their beds, he may speak in their ears and terrify them with warnings . . ." (Job 33:14–16).

The experience spoken of in this verse from Job is exactly what happened to me in the early '70s. It never happened before or since. I lived outside of Tulsa, Oklahoma, in a mobile home and attended Interstate Temple, T. L. and Daisy Osborn's church. Daisy was my Sunday school teacher, and it was in her class that I met and became friends with Margaret Hunt.

One day Margaret and her husband, Peter, announced that they were going to Nigeria, West Africa, for two years. The mission was a fulfillment of a twenty-five-year-old vision they had shared. This time they went not representing a mission board, but using their own money or donations from friends. They took their ten-year-old daughter, Elizabeth, with them.

I asked Margaret if we could correspond while she was away, and I still have all of her letters twenty-four years later. She usually wrote and asked for prayer because they were in constant danger. I sent them five or ten dollars as I could.

The urging stayed with me and became strong, but I did nothing at first.

One night I was awakened from a sound sleep and saw in a vision above me an oval-shaped, antique frame with Peter and Margaret's picture in it. I said, *"What is it, Father? Are they in danger and need prayer?"* I started praying for their safety but fell back to sleep.

Again, I was aroused and the picture was still there, but above the frame were big numbers—340. I said, *"Father, do they need money? Do You want me to send them $3.40?"*

And then, very clearly, I heard, *"There is no decimal point."*

That really woke me up, and I asked, *"Do You mean You want me to send $340?"*

Now there was only silence, so I started arguing with God saying, *"Father, You know all about me and my situation. You know that I'm alone and I have only $1,000, which will fill my propane tank for three months of winter and then I don't know what I will do. How can I send $340?"*

Then, so plainly I heard, *"Remember what I have done for you before when you obeyed Me?"*

I remembered and said, *"Yes."* I didn't argue anymore, but every day I wrestled over it. The urging stayed with me and became so strong I knew I hadn't imagined it. Then, a Christmas card came from my daughter. She and her husband were living in New Zealand, managing the Osborn's headquarters there and she knew nothing of my experience with the Lord. The card pictured a drummer boy, and she wrote, "If we give what we have to God, He can use it to feed a multitude. I love you! Merry Christmas!"

That was my confirmation! I drove to town, took $340 out of savings, wrote the check, mailed it, and said, *"OK, God, now I'll wait and see what this is all about."*

Finally, a letter came from Margaret dated March 8 that said:

> In our last letter I told you that your recent gift was an answer to prayer regarding my accompanying Peter to Liberia. I didn't go to Liberia. Peter is there now. . . . In your letter, you said you felt impressed that we might need money to come home. You were quite right. We find that we must return to the United States, quite unexpectedly. As you know, we are British . . . the American Consulate tells us that if we stay away from the States after June 30, we will lose our right to live there. . . . You, Ruth, have provided Elizabeth's fare to come home. Praise the Lord! I trust you're as excited about this miracle as we are. God saw our need long *before we knew of it.* That's just like Him, isn't it?

Wow! I learned not to argue with God. And me? Well, God sent miracles my way too. I was well taken care of before the winter was over.

Whoever can be trusted with very little can also be trusted with much, and whoever is dishonest with very little will also be dishonest with much. So if you have not been trustworthy in handling worldly wealth, who will trust you with true riches?

—Luke 16:10–11

Lord,

I know You will save me; you will not let me fall, because I trust in You.

Amen

No More Pain

By Becky Weber

Several years ago I was struck with chronic fatigue and fibromyalgia—a painful disorder of the fibrous muscle tissues. My husband had to do everything for us, including cooking and cleaning. I remember lying on the couch and crying because my body was in so much pain. If I went to the grocery store, I had to pray for help to get home. Many times I didn't have the strength to unload the groceries.

I was afraid my life was over. Infirmity and fear operated together to destroy my faith and hope. I agreed with the lie that the Lord's healing was not for me, and I was trapped in my infirmity until the Lord brought me to the point of decision. He wanted to know if I was going to believe His Word or what people were saying because of their experiences in life?

I struggled at this crossroads of faith but finally decided it wasn't up to me to decide whether or not the Lord would heal me. The Lord had called me to walk in faith and I determined to do so!

I did not receive healing instantly. It was a journey to wholeness. The Lord showed me destructive habits that needed to be changed and places in my heart that needed to be healed.

Would God heal me, or would I remain bound by fear and torment?

For years my healing continued through a peeling back of layers of destruction until the bondage of infirmity was destroyed. Gradually, the Lord built up my heart so there was no place for the spirit of infirmity and fear to remain.

One day during that time I went on a trip with a girlfriend to the Oregon coast. Because I wasn't used to driving in big cities, we decided she would drive in the Portland area. As she drove through the fast-paced traffic, I was attacked with tremendous fear. I heard a voice inside my head saying, *"I can't! I can't!"* I tried to figure out what I was afraid of. I didn't recognize that it was the voice of the spirit of fear.

Several weeks later I went to a conference in Spokane, Washington. At the end of the conference a word from the Lord was given through John Sanford. He said the Holy Spirit was delivering people from the spirit of fear. As soon as that word was spoken, a ball of Holy Spirit fire hit my chest and I began to shake all over. I felt the Lord's healing fire burning inside my whole body.

The Lord said to me, *"Becky, if you embrace this fire and let Me bring you through to the other side you will bring others through as well."*

The Lord continued to speak through John Sanford, saying that my heart and those of others had been wounded in childhood through control and criticism and that these wounds had opened a door for the spirit of fear. He said that because of this fear we were unable to fulfill the prophetic callings in our lives. I heard God say, *"I AM delivering you!"*

Then John said, "And you have heard a voice inside of your heart, saying, *'I can't! I can't,'* but the Lord this day is delivering you from that voice of fear, and you will go forward in the calling and destiny that He has intended for you!"

God impressed in my spirit, *"Becky, people who are afflicted with infirmity don't want to hear a doctrine from the Word. These wounded people need to hear that you have walked through the fire and the Lord brought you through!"*

That day I was completely healed, and I understood what God wanted me to do.

My body has been pain free for several years now! To hold my grandbabies without pain is wonderful. To cook a meal for my husband or curl my hair or walk up the stairs without pain is awesome! To simply be held by my husband without having to tell him he's hurting me is a blessing beyond words. To travel and speak in the ministry the Lord has intended for me is incredible! To know deep in my spirit that the Lord is a wonderful, loving God Who desires to restore my spirit, soul, and body is truly the greatest gift of all!

> Jesus said to the woman, "Your faith has saved you; go in peace."
>
> —Luke 7:50

Lord,

My faith comes from hearing You speak Your message to me. I hear You through the word of Christ.

Amen

Not Too Fast

By Robin Marsh

Most people think the world of a television news anchor is glamorous. The truth is, dinner between newscasts is usually determined by which drive-through line is faster. While working as the main anchor at a television station in Amarillo, Texas, I experienced a clear revelation from the Lord at, believe it or not, a fast-food restaurant. Little did I know my response that night could mean the difference between life and death for a total stranger.

My colleague and I rushed off to dinner between the 6:00 P.M. and 10:00 P.M. newscasts. We made our way to Amarillo Boulevard where one fast-food sign after another lined the street. I turned the car into our old standby, Taco Bueno. We were "looking good," made-up from head to toe in our high heels and new business suits.

As I stepped inside the restaurant door, my eyes became fixated on a man standing near us in line. This man was a mess. He reeked of alcohol and looked lonely and poor, as though he was down to his last fifty cents.

How gross! I thought.

But God instantly revealed to me that He loved this man just as much as He loved me. I felt an overwhelming voice deep inside my heart telling me to share the love of Jesus. I did not know how the stranger would respond, but I trusted the Lord to give me the words to say.

"If I buy your dinner," I said, "will you listen to what I want to share with you?"

He nodded.

I told him about the love of Christ and how Jesus died on the cross for him so he could have eternal life. I told him no matter what his circumstance, Jesus could take care of him if he would trust Him.

The man listened intently, then got his meal and sat alone to eat it. Before he left the restaurant, he returned to our table and told me no one ever had been so kind to him.

I do not know if the man made a decision for the Lord, but I left that restaurant a changed person. God humbled me and showed me that I need to be available to tell others that His grace and love is available everywhere and to everyone.

Two days later I arrived at the TV station just as I did every weekday. But the face of one of my colleagues told me something was wrong. My colleague asked me if I had heard the morning news report about a man getting killed on Amarillo Boulevard. I had seen the story but the name of the victim was not given. My heart sank when my colleague told me it was the man I had witnessed to just two nights before at the restaurant. He had stepped off the curb in front of a driver that morning and was killed instantly.

I am convinced my meeting with that man was a divine appointment. I am grateful to the Lord for teaching me about being obedient in witnessing. I hope that man and I will see each other again in heaven.

> I became a servant of this gospel by the gift of God's grace given me through the working of his power. Although I am less than the least of all God's people, this grace was given me: to preach to the Gentiles the unsearchable riches of Christ.
>
> —Ephesians 3:7–8

Lord,

Your eyes are upon the ways of man, and You see all of our steps. I set my steps to follow You.

Amen

Prayer
Weaving

By Eva Marie Everson

As a Christian writer and speaker, I was experiencing a busy time in my personal and professional life. I was stressed, overworked, underfed (who has time to eat?) and looking forward to a vacation. Actually, a nap would have been just fine, but what I really needed was a good night's sleep.

Late one night I collapsed into bed. I snuggled up to my husband's sleeping form, closed my eyes, whispered "goodnight" to my precious Lord, and willed myself to stop thinking. It was a little before midnight.

I awoke several hours later. I opened one eye, peered at the digital clock, read 4:31, and groaned. *"Lord,"* I prayed. *"Why do I have to wake so early?"*

I closed my eyes and attempted to go back to sleep, but as usual my mind began to race—thinking about one project and then another. Out of the blue, the name of a national magazine publisher came to me. I had met this one once, spoken to her a few times, and knew she lived about five miles from me, though I didn't know exactly where.

Why am I thinking about Kathleen? I wondered.

"Get up!" the Lord interrupted. *"You need to pray for Kathleen."*

Though tired, I didn't hesitate. This wasn't because I'm some spiritual giant, but because I couldn't come up with any logical reason for my being commanded to pray for a woman I barely knew. God knew something I didn't know, needed something my prayers could speak into motion. I thought I must treat this call to pray as a privilege, no matter the hour or my physical exhaustion.

I made my way into the living room where I sat on the sofa and pulled a small chenille throw over my lap in an effort to keep warm. *"Father, I don't know why you are calling me to pray for Kathleen, but, Lord, I lift her up to you now."*

"Pray for focus." The words from the Holy Spirit to my heart were direct and to the point.

Focus? Focus at work? Focus at home? I wasn't sure. *"Give her focus and direction, Lord,"* I offered.

After a few moments, the urgency to pray subsided and I returned to bed for, hopefully, a little more shut-eye.

Later that afternoon my thoughts turned toward Kathleen again. This time, I felt no call to pray, but to contact her. I called Kathleen at work, but she was too busy to chat. "May I bring something to you?" I asked. I had decided to write a letter to her about what had happened.

"Sure!" she said, giving me directions to her home.

I wrote the letter, slipped it into an envelope, sealed it, and drove the few miles to her home.

She greeted me at the door with a huge smile and said, "I'm so sorry! I'm so busy right now!"

"No, that's OK," I told her. "I'm on my way to meet my daughter for a milkshake. I just wanted you to read this." I extended the envelope, she took it, we said our good-byes, and I left.

The following day I received a call from Kathleen. "Eva Marie, I just got around to reading your letter. I just can't believe what you wrote here! I'm almost too astonished to speak!"

"Why?" I said. "What is going on?"

"As you may or may not know, I host a morning talk radio show."

"Yes, I knew that."

> *I dialed 911 on my cell phone but couldn't bring myself to press "send."*

"On my way to the station, I usually drop by the bank to make a deposit. Apparently, someone knew this and was following me yesterday morning. I sensed the danger. I reached for my cell phone, dialed 911, but couldn't bring myself to press the "send" button.

"Suddenly, a peace fell over me, blanketed my car, and I kept hearing this voice saying, *'Focus, Kathleen. Focus. Just stay focused.'* I did and somehow managed to get away from my would-be attacker. It was eerie, but at the same time I sensed something godly happening to me. Now I know! You were praying!"

Nearly a year passed before Kathleen and I saw each other again. We greeted one another with huge smiles and tight hugs. There is a bond between us that is rare and special. We are woven together with the thread of prayer, the most precious thread of all.

> Therefore let everyone who is godly pray to you while you may be found; surely when the mighty waters rise, they will not reach him.
>
> —Psalm 32:6

Lord,

You are my hiding place; You will protect me from trouble and surround me with songs of deliverance.

Amen

Warning, Plane Problems!

By Jesse Duplantis

It's fun being saved. But sometimes God will put you in funny situations *because* you are saved. For example, I was in Denver, Colorado, once waiting for a plane after preaching. I had just been to Montana, where I had preached at a college in Missoula. After that I flew to Salt Lake City, and from Salt Lake, I flew to Denver. Now I was headed to Dallas and then to New Orleans.

I didn't want to go to all those places. I just wanted to go home to New Orleans. But where the Lord calls you to go, you've got to go. So I said, "OK, Lord, I'll do it." I took the trip and was in Denver, where I was waiting for another plane to take me home. I hadn't been home in a while, and I couldn't wait to get there.

I was standing in the Denver airport waiting for them to start boarding, and I was praising God. I said to myself, *Boy, it's fun being saved. Father, I just thank You. Faith cometh by hearing and hearing by the Word of God. I hear Your Word. I read Your Word. I flow in Your anointing.*

Just then the Lord said, *"Jesse, I don't want you to get on that plane."*

I said, *"What?"*

"There will be trouble on this plane," He said. *"Don't get on it."*

"Trouble?" I asked.

God said, *"Don't get on this plane!"*

"Don't get on the plane," He said again. *"Take the next flight."*

"Huh?" I said. *"But-but, Lord, I-I'd just kind of like to go home, you know."*

"Don't get on the plane," He said, just as simply as that.

So I went over to the lady at the check-in counter and asked, "When is the next flight to Dallas?"

"Nine hours from now," she said.

When I heard her say that, I told God I didn't want to stay in the airport for nine hours.

God said, *"You can preach for nine hours. There are a lot of sinners here. You can let your light shine. Don't get on this plane. There's damage to come."*

"Man, God," I said, *"can't you just 'heal' it? At least until I get off the plane. You know, just fix it, huh?"*

"Don't!" He said. *"I'm telling you. Don't get on that plane."*

After I heard that, I had to adjust myself to staying in the airport, and I was about halfway ready when God said, *"Now, I want you to go tell that ticket agent there are problems on this plane. Tell them not to load this plane and take off."*

"God," I said, *"they're not going to listen! They're going to think I'm a fruitcake if I go up there and tell them that!"*

They're going to think I'm a fruitcake if I tell them the plane has problems!

I could see myself, saying, "Excuse me, but God told me for you all not to load this plane." You know, that sounds kind of crazy. But when you know the voice of God, you've got to do what He says. I still fought it for a few minutes before I did anything.

It was getting close to the departure time, so I knew I had to do something. I decided to walk back up to the desk and tell the lady I would take the next flight. As I got up close to the desk, I saw a guy smoking a big cigar that he'd been chewing on. It was kind of gross the way he did it. This man was sitting close to the desk, so he could hear my conversation.

I walked up really close to where he was sitting and said, "Ma'am, ah, I'm going to take the next flight out of here. Ah, I want to leave, but the Lord told me there's going to be some damage to this plane. So you might want to get another one. Don't fly this plane."

She looked at me and said, "Who told you?"

"The Lord," I said.

"The Lord who?"

"The Lord, God—Jesus," I said.

And she went, "Oh. Heh, heh, heh." She didn't believe what I was telling her.

"Lady, listen to what I'm saying," I said. "If this plane takes off, we've got problems. I'm a man of the Lord. I know you think I'm a fruitcake. I know it sounds nuts, but don't fly this plane."

"Well," she said, "we're about ready to board." She picked up the loudspeaker and called out the boarding. People started getting up to get on the plane, and the man with the cigar went over and went, "Whoof!"

I felt so stupid.

God said, *"You told them. That's all I asked you to do."*

Yeah, I told them, but they were looking at me like I was crazy. Some of the people had heard me and began to stare at me as they walked past. And that made me mad. They loaded the plane, and the devil said, *"Nine hours, my man. Nine hours. I'm going to drive you nuts for nine hours."*

The lady at the counter asked me, "Mister, are you getting on this plane?"

"Don't let that plane leave this gate," I told her. "I'm telling you, God said it. I want to go home more than anybody! I don't want to stay here nine hours. There's something wrong with this plane."

"There's nothing wrong with the plane, sir," she said. "Are you going to get on the plane, or are you going to stay here? Because if you stay, we're going to put you on standby. You may not make that flight nine hours from now either."

"No," I said. "I'm not getting on that plane."

"Fine," she said and closed the gate. *Boom!*

I was standing there, feeling like an idiot. I was outside the gate, and the devil started in on me: *"Bozo brain. Fool. You idiot."*

I joined in with him: *Boy, you're right. Huh, yeah. You're an idiot, man.*

> *The devil said, "I'm going to drive you nuts for nine hours."*

57

I sat there and watched as they pushed that plane to the runway. They fired up the engines—*zzzZZZ*. I watched it, bless God. And they got all ready to taxi down the runway. Sure enough, the engines were running—you could hear them go, *rrrRRR*. The pilot throttled it a little bit to start taxiing like he was supposed to, and he went maybe twenty-five feet before the back end of the plane just blew up. The engine on the back of the plane just blew out smoke. Something just went, *Boo-dooom!*

"Oh-hoo! Ahhhhh, yeah!" I shouted. I couldn't help it. I said, "Ha, ha, ha, look there. It's not working!"

Smoke went all over the plane, man, and people came flying down the emergency chute so fast. They were out of there! I was sitting there going, "Ha, ha, ha." I was just enjoying myself. The plane almost blew up, and I was celebrating.

Finally, they got all those people off the plane and headed back to the terminal. The people started coming back inside, and when that old boy with the cigar walked past, I just looked at him and smiled.

Within two hours they had another plane ready to fly to Dallas. And just as they started boarding, that old guy with the cigar walked up and said, "Hey, Rev., is this one OK?"

"Yes, sir," I said. "It's OK."

"What seat you got?" he asked.

"I've got 10A."

He looked at the lady behind the desk and said, "I want 10B."

I had to smell that old cigar all the way to Dallas and on to New Orleans, but it was all right because the Lord was with us.

You know, God will honor you. He will honor you when you trust Him. In fact, God honors you at the same time the devil makes you think you're the biggest idiot in town. I'm telling you, it's fun being saved! You know why it's fun being saved? Because he turns crazy situations like this one into something you can laugh about! And also because everywhere you go, God protects you.

> Whoever gives heed to instruction prospers, and blessed is he who trusts in the LORD.

> —Proverbs 16:20

Lord,

I know that You delight in my obedience more than any burnt offerings and sacrifices. Speak clearly to me that I may obey and be a delight to You.

Amen

HE LEADS US TO STILL WATERS

> He makes me lie down in [fresh, tender]
> green pastures; He leads me beside
> the still and restful waters.
>
> **—Psalm 23:2 AMP**

Shepherds lead their sheep to drink from still waters, because if sheep fall into a fast current their wool would easily become waterlogged and cause them to drown. Likewise, the Lord leads us to simple truths when we are at risk of drowning in our fears, ambitions, or anxieties.

My friend and volunteer smokejumper, Stan Tate, tells many stories about fighting fires in the mountains of Idaho that amaze his audiences with the sense of beauty he also enjoyed in the dangerous forces of nature. Gratefully, we needn't parachute from an airplane to enjoy the mountain pastures he describes in, "Surprised by Joy." Cecil Murphey went all the way to Kenya to learn the valuable lesson on giving and receiving—a lesson we can all remember from now on.

Regardless of whether our storms are stirred by health problems, career changes, loneliness, or lost toys, the Lord cares about our anxieties and is present to peacefully lead us to His place of refreshment. And as Joyce Meyer testifies in her story titled, "Chopped Fruit," sometimes our greatest refreshment comes when we refresh others.

Surprised by Joy

By Stan Tate

Idaho smokejumpers—firefighters who parachute into forests to suppress forest fires—have a deep fear of having to parachute on the rim of Hells Canyon. It is a deeper gorge than Grand Canyon with similar walls of rock. Late one summer my greatest fear became a reality. I was chosen to jump on a small fire on the rugged side of Hells Canyon.

Shell Oil Company was filming our jump, so that was one consolation. As our aircraft circled the jump spot, which was a quarter mile above the fire, I was terrified as I looked down at the formidable canyon. The man who told us when and where to exit the plane decided the wind was blowing toward the east, and we had to jump out directly above the Snake River, 6,000 feet below.

I thought my partner was half submerged in oscillating shallow water.

My partner jumped first and spiraled down toward a small meadow beside a blue lake. The unforgiving wind carried him right above the lake. He landed in the middle of it and then stood up in the shallow water, waving a banner that he was all right.

The spotter told me to avoid hitting the water but land in the meadow. I bailed out above the river and headed for the meadow. About 500 feet above a clearing amid the huge cliffs, my partner shouted up to me to land where he did. I circled over it and was hit with an aroma like the fragrance of a San Francisco floral shop. I thought my partner was half submerged in the oscillating shallow water below.

By then I couldn't avoid hitting the water. To my amazement, it wasn't water but a natural pasture of blue lupine waving in the strong breeze. Soaring like a bird, I caught a celestial glimpse of God's glorious creation. I landed in this floral garden surrounded by a field of wildflowers as tall as my waist. I felt like I had dropped into the Garden of Eden—everything was perfect. Two white-tailed deer stood beside us, wondering what we were doing.

I thanked Almighty God for changing my greatest fear into one of my most profound moments of exhilaration and joy. Sometimes our worst fears turn into our greatest accomplishments. When we believe in God we are constantly surprised by joy.

Let the heavens rejoice, let the earth be glad; let them say among the nations, "The LORD reigns!" Let the sea resound, and all that is in it; let the fields be jubilant, and everything in them!

—1 Chronicles 16:31–32

Lord,

I give You praise, for You have granted peace in the land, and no one makes me afraid. Your abundance satisfies me and Your presence assures me of Your love. You have walked with me and been my God, and I will be Your child.

Amen

Remembering and Forgetting

By Cecil Murphey

"They could have at least thanked me," I grumbled. A family had needed help and several of us had given them food, clothes, and money. The husband had started a new job, and we provided for them until he got his first paycheck.

A few days before I left for a visit to Kenya, I went by their house to give them telephone numbers of people to contact. That's when I found out they had moved. When I had been there two days earlier, the wife had said nothing about their coming departure.

"Ungrateful!" My voice echoed through the empty, filthy rooms. "We did so much for them, and this is the way they treat us. They could have at least thanked me."

Although I knew my attitude wasn't right, I resented their lack of appreciation. When I thought of the time and the effort I had put into helping them, anger raced through my heart. *"Help me understand, God, and enable me to release this resentment,"* I prayed.

For the next several days I continued to brood over their lack of appreciation. Then I pushed aside my anger because I needed to focus on my trip to Kenya, where I had served six years as a missionary.

A dozen years had passed since my family and I had returned to the United States. I wondered if I would recognize people, and I worried that I'd forgotten the language. But all my concerns disappeared when five African pastors met my plane. Within seconds I felt utterly comfortable with them— like old times.

For the next ten days we traveled extensively. I visited churches I had helped start and talked to congregations I'd preached to twelve years before. It was a wonderful time of reconnecting with old friends.

The night before I was to leave for America, I met with nine pastors in a remote area near Lake Victoria in the home of one of the pastors, Blasio Were. Blasio's wife served a wonderful dinner, and afterwards we sat around the table and reminisced as sunset approached.

Turning to Erastus, who sat next to me, I told him how grateful I was to him for teaching me the tribal language—Luo. "I don't know how I would have learned Luo if you hadn't worked so hard to teach me," I said.

"I did very little," he said. "A lesson or two, that was all."

"A few lessons? You did more than that." In those days, Erastus had been a teacher in an elementary school twelve miles away. As soon as he finished his classes, he got on his bicycle and rode to the compound where I lived. Most afternoons, he spent at least an hour teaching me.

"If you say that is true, it must be so," he said, "but I do not remember being of much help to you."

"How could you not remember?" I said.

A few minutes later Nathaniel Jullu said, "Do you remember the financial problems I had after I became a pastor?" Nathaniel had left teaching and started a church. "My wife had no money and the offerings were too small. I borrowed money from you to pay for my children's school fees."

"You did?" I asked.

"You do not remember? How can that be so? And when I could not repay, you said that you had canceled my debt. I shall always remember."

Just before the final rays of light vanished, Blasio left the room and returned with a Petromax—a German-made, kerosene-operated, pressure lamp. He hung it on a rope suspended from the ceiling.

"Neh (look)." He pointed to the lamp and smiled.

I smiled back. "Nice lamp." Then I returned to the conversation with the others. The tales again poured out. I reminded another pastor of the time he had volunteered to travel two days by bus to Kisumu (125 miles away) to buy a part for my motorcycle. "You stay and teach; I will go for you," he had said.

"Did I do that?" he asked and shrugged as if it were nothing.

Blasio patiently listened to the conversation, but he said nothing more. Several times a frown crossed his face. Finally, he pointed to the Petromax again. "Neh! Mano ber? (Look, isn't it nice?)"

"Yes, it's very nice," I answered in Luo. "You keep it spotless and that lamp provides a lot of light. That's the kind of lamp I used when we lived upcountry. They give the most light."

"No! No!" Blasio said in Luo. "Not because I keep it shined. It is because it is *the* lamp. Look, can you not see that?" He touched the Petromax and stroked it affectionately. "This is the lamp you gave me."

"I did?" I had absolutely no recollection of having done that.

"Before you moved to the coast, you gave this lamp to me. You said you would not need it because they have electricity there. Other missionaries sold their goods, but you *gave* this to me."

"You've kept it looking nice," I said, wondering why he wouldn't drop the subject.

> *God spoke to me from the mouth of an uneducated African.*

Blasio shook his head and gazed into space. Although he was a pastor, he had little formal education—probably three years in school at most. He was the only one in the room who didn't speak fluent English, which was why we had kept the conversation in the tribal language.

"You gave this very one to me," he said. "You had been to my house and saw that I possessed only a small lamp. 'This will give you more light,' you said to me. Do you not remember?"

I shook my head and tried to move the conversation to another subject.

Blasio stared into infinity for several minutes before he jumped up. He rushed over, threw his arms around me, and smiled. "Ah, yes, this is the way of God, is it not?"

"What do you mean?" I asked.

"You have done acts of kindness for these my brothers and you do not remember, is that not so? And they have done acts of kindness for you that they can no longer remember, right?"

"Yes—"

"Ah, yes, they remember what you have done. You remember what they have done. Ah, this is the way God teaches us, is it not?"

I still didn't understand.

Blasio stared at me with dark, glowing eyes. "At last I have understood this about the way of God. Those who give must never remember. Those who receive must never forget. Is that not the way of God?"

His words stunned me. I nodded. My mind slid back to the incident just before I left the United States. God had spoken to me through the mouth of Blasio. I had heard exactly the message I needed.

Not only had I remembered my generosity, but I had expected that family I'd helped back home to thank me. I had been wrong. I had given my gifts to God, not to them. I had done what I had felt God wanted me to do. It was no longer any of my business whether they thanked me or not. My task was to forget; it would be up to God to make them remember.

"I have learned an important lesson from you," I told Blasio. "I had to travel thousands of miles to hear it, and I promise you, it is a lesson I will not forget."

And I still remember.

> But when you give to the needy, do not let your left
> hand know what your right hand is doing, so that

your giving may be in secret. Then your Father, who
sees what is done in secret, will reward you.

—Matthew 6:3–4

Lord,

*Give me a heart that loves others with
Your passion, for I could give all I possess
to the poor and surrender my body to the
flames, but if I have not love,
I gain nothing.*

Amen

My Real Life Miracle

By Tedi E. Martin

On December 12, 2000, I was diagnosed with a cranial nerve tumor. I immediately began seeking medical help and went to three neurosurgeons and a neurologist. All four confirmed that I would need to have the tumor surgically removed because it was on a nerve. They told me that it was a rare tumor because of its location and that I would need a specialist to do the operation and a neurosurgeon to assist.

I was to have a second MRI on March 19. The neurosurgeon who was to perform the operation wanted to take another look at the tumor to see how they should enter my skull.

My church family had constantly lifted my need before the Lord. On Sunday, March 18, the elders of my church prayed for my healing, following the example in James 5:14. This was a beautiful, God-honoring prayer. My father was among those who laid hands on me and prayed. It meant so much to me to have him there for that prayer.

We didn't know what the outcome would be, but we did know that we were doing what God had told us to do in His Word. We were of one spirit in this prayer. During the prayer, I kept saying over and over again, *"Lord, help my unbelief. Lord, help my unbelief,"* just as the man in Mark 9:24 had asked of Jesus. We knew that God would be faithful to hear our prayer.

On Monday I went for the MRI and to hear the results from the doctor. The receptionist led Mother, Dad, Ron, and me into the examining room where we waited and waited and waited. I'm used to waiting in a doctor's office, but not after I'd been put in the examining room, so we wondered why it was taking so long.

Finally, my doctor came in, put the scan up on the light, and said, "It's gone! It's not there."

I jumped off of the table and went to get a closer look. I could hear Mother, Dad, and Ron praising God and sobbing behind me. I dropped to my knees and looked at my doctor who was seated on a small stool beside the scan and said, "You do remember me, don't you? (I had only seen him once before, so I wanted to be sure he didn't have me mixed up with another patient.) You remember that I had a tumor on the cranial nerve, don't you?"

"Oh, yes," he said. "I remember you and I know it was there, but it's not there anymore."

He told us that we had to wait so long because he had called the imaging center to have them look at the original film and to tell him that they had not made a mistake; he wanted to confirm that the tumor was not there. And the radiologist, who is a medical doctor himself, did confirm—the tumor was not there!

We left the surgeon's office and went straight to the church. We wanted to tell our pastor immediately how God had answered our prayers and that He truly had performed a miracle. The pastor was as overjoyed and humbled as we were.

We bowed our heads in thanksgiving for our glorious God, Who allowed us to experience such a beautiful miracle.

> They will tell of the power of your awesome works, and I will proclaim your great deeds. They will celebrate your abundant goodness and joyfully sing of your righteousness.

> —Psalm 145:6–7

Lord,

But You, O Sovereign Lord, deal well with me for Your name's sake; out of the goodness of Your love, deliver me.

Amen

Not Forgotten

By Charles Joulwan

I worked with a particular inmate named Tim for a few years in the prison. One day he said he was being released. He told me that he'd never forget how I helped him in many ways and that I was like a father to him. Once he was released I never saw him. One week, two weeks, three weeks went by and no Tim!

Then on the third Sunday I had just arrived home from the prison and was about to go into the house when the Spirit impressed me to go get the Sunday paper out of my box.

I was tired and said, *"I'll get it later."*

The Spirit persisted.

I went and got the paper.

Meanwhile, some of Tim's neighbors had taken him to church and on their way home he realized they were in the neighborhood where I lived. Right away Tim started praying, *"Lord, I need to see Chaplain Charlie. I promised him that I wouldn't forget him."*

Just as he finished praying, he looked up and saw me walking back to the house with the Sunday paper! He couldn't believe his eyes. "Turn around!" he shouted to the people in the car. "That's Chaplain Charlie!"

Tim hopped out of the car and ran up to me. We hugged. He told me how he was doing, and we still correspond today.

Ask and it will be given to you; seek and you will find; knock and the door will be opened to you.

—Matthew 7:7

Lord,

I praise You that You give good gifts to Your children. Thank You for opening the door of blessings for me.

Amen

Cody's Perfect Prayer

By Armené Humber

Cody was born perfect. But, while he was still a baby, his father slammed his tiny body against a wall in a moment of rage. Branded forever with both mental and physical impairment, Cody could speak only garbled words and needed braces to walk. Even then, he could only maneuver on level surfaces.

The summer Cody turned ten he was given a wonderful opportunity to go to camp. It was a special camp where all the children had old wounds inflicted by grownups, but whose scars were not all so visible as Cody's. Here Cody's social workers hoped he could begin to learn that there were adults he could trust. The camp staff prayed that, somehow, he could encounter his heavenly Father and begin to believe how very much he was loved.

Camp would be an enormous hurdle for Cody. For an entire week, he would live on the mountain with a counselor he did not know and a camper-buddy he had never met. Like any first-time camper, he was both hyper-excited and terribly frightened. Cody's fear, rooted in the sharp reality of past experience, haunted him with endless questions. What would his counselor be like? Would he hurt Cody when he got tired of him? Would he make sure he had enough to eat? Would he get angry if Cody got scared in the middle of the night?

Who could handle the challenge of Cody's care? Would Cody understand God's love?

While Cody worried over every fear, the camp staff wondered how, in five short days, they could meet the daunting challenge of caring for him in a rough camp environment while convincing him of God's enormous love. Because of his impairments, Cody would need a counselor who was strong enough to push him up and down steep trails in a wheelbarrow—the only way they could think to transport him around camp—yet gentle enough to care for his soul. Finally, they decided. If anyone could handle the challenge, it was Dan.

All week Dan pushed Cody up steep hills and over bumpy trails. To the swimming pool and the dining hall. To the craft center and bunk hall. He lifted him in and out of bed and dressed him. He helped him with his braces and with his meals. He leaned patiently into every labored word Cody spoke in an effort to understand him. He never left

Cody's side. All the while he prayed that every Bible story and verse he read would spark Cody's interest. But there was nothing from Cody—not a clue—to let Dan know he was getting through. Each day Dan wavered between hope and doubt that Cody could believe God loved him.

By the end of the week, Dan's knee was protesting and he was limping in pain. Wincing, he kept on—pushing Cody's wheelbarrow, feeding him, refusing to hand his care to anyone else, praying all the while that Cody could grasp how very much God loved him, and asking God to show him somehow that Cody heard. But time was short. The week was almost over.

On the final evening at camp, Dan bowed his head with his two campers for their last bedtime prayers together. Cody was quiet as Dan gently spoke a compassionate prayer for each of their lives. But as he finished, Dan felt a slight tugging at his sleeve. Looking down at Cody's upturned face, he realized Cody wanted to pray too. He was surprised, but nodded and waited patiently.

Carefully, Cody bowed his head, folded his hands, and struggled to form his prayer. Very slowly, he pushed four twisted words from his mouth.

"God . . . Dan . . . knee . . . please."

Suddenly Dan understood what God had known all along—Cody *had* encountered God's love in every moment of that week. It had pushed him in the wheelbarrow and lifted him in and out of bed. It had not dropped him or hurt him. It had never let him go when he got heavy. It had stood patiently by his bed in the middle of the night to comfort him through his nightmares. All week long God had poured soothing comfort and healing salve into the holes in Cody's soul, slowly sealing them up until, finally, Cody could sense God's love welling inside of him.

Now, from this small beginning pool of love and trust, Cody drew out just enough to offer back to Dan. And in those four imperfect words, Dan heard Cody's perfect prayer.

"Please, God, heal Dan's hurt, just like you are healing mine."

> Be devoted to one another in brotherly love. Honor one another above yourselves. Never be lacking in zeal, but keep your spiritual fervor, serving the Lord. Be joyful in hope, patient in affliction, faithful in prayer. Share with God's people who are in need. Practice hospitality.
>
> —Romans 12:10–13

Lord,

You have said that to love others is to love You. I desire to bring good and not harm to my neighbors. Show me ways to be hospitable so that I will bring glory to You.

Amen

One Fateful Night

By Michael R. Wells

One day when I was a young Christian, I accepted a promotion with a major retailer. I had been waiting to be offered a management trainee position and now I finally had been given my chance. There was one catch, however. I would have to move from my home in Spokane, Washington, to Fairbanks, Alaska, at my own expense. I had accepted the position believing that it was God's will but had avoided asking counsel from any spiritual adviser.

That evening I went to a small prayer meeting I'd been attending for the past four months or so. I had accepted Christ as my Savior and been filled with the Holy Spirit at one of the earlier meetings. When I arrived I learned that the leaders had decided to drop the usual prayer meeting format and have a Bible study. I can't recall the theme of the teaching, but I remember it zeroed in on good reasons why I should not have accepted my new job. To my knowledge there was no way the person giving the study could have known I'd been offered and accepted a promotion earlier that day.

I remember thinking, *Why can't they be happy about my getting the job of my dreams? It's my right to choose where I work, isn't it? So what's the big deal?*

Was I headed for destruction and loss like Lot experienced?

As I rode home with my friend Randy, I challenged the verses and logic presented in the study, but my faithful friend wouldn't agree with me. Before we parted I asked him what I should do, and he encouraged me to seek God's solution to my dilemma.

Early the next morning I got up and prayed. It was my day off but I could not sleep in. I knew I had to find out God's will. I was led to read in Genesis and I happened on the story of Abraham and Lot in chapter 13. I saw that dissension caused these two men to part.

My heart was pierced. I wondered, *Have I chosen my own way just as Lot did? Am I headed for the valley of Sodom and Gomorrah and all the loss Lot suffered there?* I could not yield, however, to what I had begun to sense. But I kept praying, out of fear if nothing else.

About an hour later my sister-in-law arrived. To get a visit from her was very unusual.

"So what brings you by?" I asked.

"I just thought I should stop by," she said, "so I did."

Only two weeks before she had been baptized in the Holy Spirit at one of the same prayer meetings I'd attended the night before. I began telling her about how I believed God had shown me in Genesis that I was not to go to Alaska.

"Genesis!" she said. "Why, the Lord woke me around five this morning and He spoke the word *'Genesis'* to me. When I asked what chapter, He said, *'chapter 13.'* Then I asked what verse and He ran off a whole bunch of verses."

What was I to say? I had intentionally avoided telling her what chapter I was referring to, but she knew about it even before I did. God had used her to confirm that He was speaking to me. However, I still wasn't willing to leave my dreams behind. What was I going to tell my mom who was excited about my new opportunity? And how about my store manager; hadn't he gone out of his way to get me the job? What would he think of me when I told him God told me to refuse the promotion?

It was now Thursday night and time for another prayer meeting at church. All through the service I vacillated. Should I keep the job or yield to what God was saying?

By the conclusion of the service I decided to see if I could get another confirmation of God's leading. I sought out a trusted church elder named Ron. He had a strong and proven prophetic gift. I told him all about the promotion and how my sister-in-law had confirmed what God had been telling me in Genesis. I told Ron everything, that is, except that my heart was pierced by God when I realized that dissension had caused Abraham and Lot to part company. Secretly, I worried that dissension could cause God and me to part also.

As Ron laid his hands on my shoulders and prepared to pray, he began to thank the Lord for answering my request for guidance. His eyes were shut tight. Suddenly, he took his hands off me, looked me straight in the eye, and said, "I don't think there's a need to pray any further. I believe the Lord has given me the key to your problem. Just now the Spirit spoke the word *'dissension'* to me. Does this word mean anything to you?" he asked.

I was undone. Amazingly, the only piece of information that I had withheld had been revealed to one of God's faithful servants. There could now be no more doubt as to what God's intentions were for me. All I had to do was choose to follow his will, and I did.

The next day I told my store manager that I really appreciated all he'd done for me but I'd decided to decline the job offer. My mother cried when she learned of my decision. All she wanted was the best for me but at the time she couldn't understand why her son would refuse such a wonderful opportunity.

This September it will be twenty-eight years since that fateful night when a prayer meeting was turned over to the Holy Spirit and a tidal wave of divine intervention arose to save a wandering son. All I can say is thank heaven for all the faithful servants who responded promptly when God told them what to do. I am convinced that without the unbroken chain of events that concluded with the word of knowledge given by my friend Ron, my life might well have ended up just like Lot's life.

Nine months after refusing the Fairbanks position, the same retailer offered me a management trainee job. I accepted the position and began work in a brand new store in downtown Spokane. God is truly faithful!

> But if he will not listen, take one or two others along,
> so that every matter may be established by the testi-
> mony of two or three witnesses.
>
> —Matthew 18:16

Lord,

I can say with confidence that You are my helper; I will not be afraid. You are with me each step of the way!

Amen

$\mathcal{P}$utting

Down
$\mathcal{R}$oots

By Margolyn Woods

"I don't want to do the first grade over!" Taryn screamed. "They'll call me stupid!"

My whole being ached for my seven-year-old daughter. "It's not your fault," I said. "Oklahoma schools are further ahead than your Idaho school."

We had moved five times in Taryn's short life and each transplant seemed to steal away more of my daughter's security and joy. Roy, my husband, and I had done all we could, like making sure she had familiar things around her and giving her lots of attention. We even bought some sheep to put in the big red barn on our

Oklahoma property. But having to do the first grade over again was the last straw.

As the first day of school drew closer Taryn became more and more withdrawn. Depression welled up inside me as Taryn pulled into herself more with each passing day.

One evening as Taryn and I put the sheep in the barn for the night, Taryn gave Crystal, a pretty white-faced sheep, some extra food. Crystal was always the last sheep to arrive for dinner, but Taryn didn't mind.

The vet said it looked like hoof rot. The whole herd was at risk.

"That's all right," she said, stroking Crystal's neck. "I saved some just for you."

Maybe . . . maybe this sheep is what she needs, I thought.

Several weeks later, Taryn came running to the house, "Mommy, Mommy, come quick, Crystal is hurt!"

Oh no, I thought. *Why Crystal?*

Our visiting vet examined her and sounded grim, "It looks like hoof rot, a disease that can easily take down a whole herd," she announced. "I'm going to show you how to administer some antibiotics, Mrs. Woods, and I'll check back with you next week."

Then she handed me some medicine and syringes. For the next seven days, I wrestled that 180-pound sheep, sat on her, and gave her the medicine. The following Wednesday, the doctor returned.

"I'm sorry," she said. "I'm afraid there isn't much change. My suggestion would be to put her down so as not to infect the rest of the herd."

Taryn's scream tore my heart.

The doctor looked away and then said, "Well, there is a veterinary school about eighty miles from here. You might have them take a look at her. But," she added, "please understand . . . there isn't much hope."

I made an appointment for the following morning. The problem, however, was getting her there. We took out the seats in my van and lined the floor with plastic. Then Roy and I lifted Crystal into the van and halter-tied her. Driving through the gate, I waved good-bye to Roy, Taryn, and our twin boys.

What have I gotten myself into? I thought as I headed onto the freeway. Five miles down the road, I was startled by an eerie sound from the back of the van.

"Baa! Baa!" Crystal bleated.

Glancing in my rearview mirror, I saw terror in the eyes of a normally docile sheep.

"Crystal," I tried to soothe, "it's OK. You're going to be all right."

Suddenly, an unpleasant odor hit me in the front part of the van, and for the next hour and a half I drove with all of the windows down, and my head hanging out the window.

"God," I pleaded, *"You know what this sheep means to Taryn, please let her be OK."*

As I entered the gates to the large animal hospital, students directed me to the unloading shoot, where I hurriedly opened the back doors of my van. If those students were shocked at the condition on the inside of the van, they didn't let it show. With reassuring voices and affectionate pats, they helped me move Crystal into the shoot.

While waiting for the doctor, I sank my fingers deep into her coarse, oily wool to reach the smooth skin on her neck. She felt hot, and I wondered if she was fevered or if she had simply worked herself into a frenzy.

"*God, please let there be a way to help her,*" I prayed.

The doctor interrupted my prayers. "If you would like to have a seat in the waiting room, Mrs. Woods, I'll talk to you after we've opened up this foot."

The young surgeon's face was smiling as he stepped into the waiting room an hour later. "We had to remove more than half of her foot, but Crystal should be just fine," he said. He handed me seven days worth of medication and syringes.

As they helped me load Crystal into the van and I saw her look at me with recognition, tears filled my eyes. Crystal was just as nervous on the trip home as she had been earlier, but I couldn't help smiling. I remem-

> *Crystal looked at me and I understood God's shepherding care for His sheep.*

bered all the times in the Bible when God calls us his sheep. I had always pictured Him looking at a flock of sheep, but these last few months had changed that image. Each of my sheep is different, just as each person is different. And God cares about each and every one of us as I care about Crystal.

As the van bounced toward our barn, I saw Roy and three smiling children's faces, but I was drawn to my little girl, jumping up and down, so happy and so full of life. What answered prayer!

Taryn parked herself in the corner of Crystal's stall for the rest of the afternoon. "It's going to be OK," she cooed. "I'll take care of you."

That evening I walked out to the barn to check on Crystal. When I opened the barn door, she stopped eating and looked up at me with eyes so trusting that I felt my throat tighten and my eyes well up. *The way a sheep looks at a shepherd*, I thought.

We've put down roots in Oklahoma and we hope to stay. Taryn and I are content. But I know that the Lord is our dwelling place and wherever we wander we'll be home, under the watchful eye of our Shepherd.

> I will save you; you will not fall by the sword but will escape with your life, because you trust in me, declares the LORD.

> —Jeremiah 39:18

Let the morning bring me word of Your unfailing love, for I have put my trust in You. Show me the way I should go, for to You I lift up my soul.

God Hears

BY JOY DEKOK

Looking out my kitchen window, I watched my husband and thirteen-year-old nephew, Kevin, climb a ladder to the garage roof.

"Um, guys, what are you doing up there?" I asked, standing in the yard below them.

"Kevin's plane landed somewhere in the woods," my husband said. The two males took turns with the binoculars while they discussed how high the air-propelled plane had been flying, the wind speed, and the direction it was going when they lost sight of it. About the size of a crow, painted bright purple and yellow, it should have been easy to spot.

Half an hour later Kevin and my husband climbed down without having sighted the missing plane. Kevin did his best to accept the loss, but I could tell he was sad.

"Well, one cool thing happened," Kevin said.

"What?" I asked.

"We could look right into a robin's nest with the binoculars."

I woke up the next morning determined to find the plane. We could go to town and buy another one, but this one was special to Kevin. I felt compelled to hunt. With ten acres of woods, I knew the search could take awhile. Kevin and I stood at the edge of the trees and I prayed, "God, You know where this plane is and how important it is to us. Please show me the way."

> *I felt compelled to hunt for the plane, but with ten acres of woods it wouldn't be easy.*

I stepped into the woods. Glancing back at Kevin, I saw a mixture of hope and doubt on his face. I pushed my way through wild raspberry bushes and dense underbrush. About twenty feet into the woods, I saw the plane jammed about waist high into brush against a tree.

"I found it!" I yelled.

Kevin responded with joyful shout. He came into the woods before I could free the plane from the brush. He examined it and showed me a bit of damage on the wing, assuring me it could still fly.

Later the same day Kevin went out to fly his big Styrofoam glider. I looked out the kitchen window a few moments later and saw him looking up into a huge oak tree—shoulders slumped, empty-handed. Tight in the top branches rested the glider. I joined him at the base of the tree. We didn't own a ladder tall enough and the steep hillside beside the tree made it an unsafe spot to set a ladder anyway. The air was still and heavy with humidity.

I put my arm around Kevin's shoulders and whispered, "Please Lord, one more time." A gentle breeze blew across the yard, and we watched the glider lift and then float to the lawn undamaged. As Kevin picked it up, the air again became still.

Kevin is now sixteen and beginning glider pilot training. As he soars with the eagles, he can remember looking into a robin's nest and knowing God heard our prayers and answered.

> He makes clouds rise from the ends of the earth; he sends lightning with the rain and brings out the wind from his storehouses.
>
> —Psalm 135:7

Lord,

I will give You thanks, for You answered me.

Amen

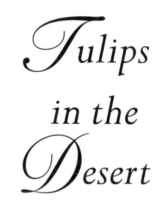

Tulips in the Desert

The story behind the song
"I Love You, Lord"

By Laurie Klein

I f you've ever wakened at 3:00 A.M. to the sound of dueling cats beneath a metal trailer propped on cinder blocks, you'd understand my fear—surely, *this* was the end of the world. That's how life felt in 1974, the year of motherhood and spiritual wilderness, the year I first planted bulbs.

My mother had mailed a dozen Red Emperors to me to brighten our low desert landscape. I had to ask which end of the tulip bulbs went up. But I planted them.

My days were flooded with sameness. I had a husband in school full time and a toddler who was busy all the time. *I'll find a life again*, I told myself. *Sometime.*

Meanwhile, we rented a trailer in Bend, Oregon. It was a small, silvery ark in a sea of sagebrush. Daily the dust seeped through ill-fitting windows, hiding the brooding mountain trinity of The Three Sisters west of town. Instead of allowing me to see the mountains, my windows opened on gravel-spitting semitrailers and tumbleweed.

> *I sought God. What I found was mostly wind and that infernal dust.*

Since we had no friends, money, or church home I spent the baby's rare nap times outside, working beneath sky too wide and beside a highway too loud and long for walks with a stroller. Because I didn't drive, I had no escape.

So I labored out there, refinishing cast-off family antiques. I'd inherited Great-Grandma's fifty-cent oak chairs from Sears and Roebuck. Paint remover ate through my cheap, cotton gloves, burning my skin. But gold glimmered through the blistering film of blackened varnish and gave me hope.

I began my mornings by the window with my Bible and guitar. I sought even the slightest variations in emptiness, reasoning that what appeared barren might become openness, a doorway through desert. With all my heart I sought God. What I heard was mostly wind and that infernal dust sifting through the cracks.

Now I know that I needed to let the wilderness—both physical and spiritual—simply happen to me, embrace the limitations, the loneliness and poverty, the silence, the bare bones of it. But I was twenty-four. I had not yet learned to wait.

Every morning without fail I had devotions. I embroidered pillows with junk-store burlap and yarn remnants. I grew things. I wrote songs. I played and read with our daughter. We ate endless beans, grilled cheese, oatmeal, and eggs. On a good day we had soup, steamed from those distressed vegetables always marked down at the market. And the week's highlight? Family treks through Bi-Mart where for forty-nine cents you could buy a plant, something alive to bring back home.

But for all my efforts, I felt my good Christian inside died a little. I was frustrated, moody, impatient. How does one fathom a Father Who allures you into wilderness, as Hosea says, so he can speak tenderly to you?

I stopped fighting deprivation the morning I embraced Psalm 131. It recommends "a soul quieted like a weaned child with its mother." I'd nursed our baby; I understood the image. I even made a song out of it, so I wouldn't forget.

But another week of quietness passed with no sense of God meeting me. *He's awfully busy,* I reasoned, *maybe He forgot.*

Strolling outdoors, I discovered the first green tulip leaves pricking through snow. I thought about Isaiah 62 where the land named Desolate becomes God's delight. *Will I ever bloom here?*

I don't know why I bothered taking my guitar from its case the day I hit bottom—habit, I suppose. *"Lord,"* I prayed, *"I've got nothing left to say, nor the heart to sing it if I did. If you want music, you'll have to give me something you want to hear."*

Aimlessly strumming a new progression I'd learned, I found words and melody welling: "I love you, Lord, and I lift my voice to worship you, oh my soul, rejoice!"

If there was one thing I'd yearned for—aside from a new life—it was to bless my Father. Even if I were struck blind or mute, I wanted God to read my actions, my body language as praise.

Because the words I'd just sung seemed to capture that prayer, I jotted them down, not sure I could even repeat the music. But I did, and the final lines came to me like a present. "Take joy, my king, in what you hear; let me be a sweet, sweet sound in your ear."

As an artist, it's continually humbling to know your best work occurred half a lifetime ago, and whose ongoing anointing has nothing to do with you. It's also a privilege. Even though the Lord sent my song to the nations, that day it was private, as beautiful as tall, red tulips in a wasteland—a simple gift that changed everything absolutely.

> I will lead her into the desert . . . and will make the Valley of Achor [trouble] a door of hope. There she will sing.
>
> —Hosea 2:14b–15a

Lord,

How precious also are Your thoughts to me, O God! How great is the sum of them! If I should count them, they would be more in number than the sand; when I awake, I am still with You.

Amen

The Higher Power

By Karen Bean

"*Don't carry out the clinics the way you always have. I have arranged the team to be divisible by three. Divide up into the three vans and listen as I direct you to those who are crying out to hear of Me.*" These were the directions the Lord clearly gave on our fifth medical trip.

This was our third mission to Kenya, but our first clinic in Maasailand. The well-trained team of eighteen knew what we were doing and how to work together. We had always set up a clinic and let the people come to us. Why change? "If it ain't broke don't fix it."

I hated this attitude in others when *I* wanted to try something new, but now the shoe was on the other foot. But being obedient, the next morning we loaded the vans and departed in three different directions as the Lord guided us. The Holy Spirit gave each member of our van a piece of information and ensured there was no "spiritual guru" among us. We were a team and God continued to show us this by alternately telling each of us which way we were to go.

Our direction? Go to the other side of a mountain range to reach people who were waiting to hear of Jesus. The Spirit of God gave us directions to leave the highway on the next small road to the left, then proceed right at a fork. Thinking this was an uninhabited swamp, the driver was shocked as we passed many people and *bomas*, which are Maasai villages containing dung huts and surrounded by a briar fence. We traveled on what would be the equivalent of a cow trail, mere ruts, until the Lord directed us to climb a big hill. As we topped the rise, a large boma lay ahead of us.

> *The Spirit of God told us to take the small road toward what the driver thought was a swamp.*

At the shock of seeing the large, metal "animal" with white-skinned inhabitants drive in, the people ran to the safety of their boma. Our Maasai interpreter translated our words exactly to the man who stood guard near the opening, *"We have come to tell you about Jesus, the Son of God."*

People started yelling, waving their arms, and running excitedly out of the boma, heading in all directions. I jumped out of the van to make sure they understood we weren't there to hurt but to help them. An explanation was interpreted back: They were not frightened. They wanted to hear and were running to get all the others. We were to wait. People seemed to run in from everywhere. They gathered patiently under a tree, but they were obviously excited. Finally, we could begin.

A member of our group preached a simple and clear message and then invited the people to receive Jesus as their Savior. When all hands went up I instructed the interpreter to reexplain the invitation. I couldn't believe *all* the Maasai wanted to receive Christ. But each person declared they had never accepted Jesus and desired to do so now.

One of the men, Joseph, told us he and another man had been sent to a school to learn to read. I asked if this was where they originally heard the gospel.

Joseph said, "We did not know there were other people. We thought this valley was all there was. We have not seen people with skin as yours. We knew there had to be a Higher Power to create all the beauty and the order in nature. We met to discuss this and decided our main goal was to find this Higher Power. We all searched. One day as one of the warriors was walking in the jungle he found this."

He showed me a leather-bound, red-letter edition Bible. I was surprised because we had stopped at several Christian bookstores in Nairobi to purchase Bibles in the Maasai language but were told that Maasais were not receptive and few could read so they didn't stock them anymore.

Proudly displaying the Bible, Joseph explained that the warrior thought this object *was* the Higher Power since he had been hoping to find Him. When the warrior brought his treasure to the elders, Joseph explained that it was a book and it had words. From that point every morning they gathered under the tree—the very tree under which we had shared the gospel. And they read from "The Book."

They read, "In the beginning God created the heaven and earth." They discovered the Higher Power had a name—God. Later they learned people could talk to God, so once a week they talked to Him.

Their prayer?

"Send someone to tell us about You."

Thus, when we arrived with the statement, "We have come to tell you about Jesus, the Son of God," they knew God had answered their prayers.

Joseph asked, "What means pastor?"

Since the Maasai believe they are the owners of all cattle I was not sure if he meant pasture or pastor so I asked him to explain.

He told me he kept hearing words in his chest that said, *"You are pastor of these people."*

I knew God was speaking to him! We made sure Joseph received proper training and mentoring.

After the whole tribe prayed to receive Christ as Savior, we treated their physical needs by giving necessary medications, vitamins, and toothbrushes.

In that short week through the travels of these three vans at least seven different groups who were seeking truth were told about Jesus for the first time. They had different names for God such as "The Great One" and "The Beginner of All Things." God knew the heart of these simple people and sent a team from across the world to show and tell them about the One they were seeking, the One with the highest power.

Today a church stands in this area on the other side of the mountain. Pastor Joseph teaches from the Bible about God and His Son, Jesus Who is, indeed, the Higher Power.

> Because that which may be known of God is manifest in them; for God hath shewed it unto them. For the invisible things of him from the creation of the world are clearly seen, being understood by the things that are made, even his eternal power and Godhead; so that they are without excuse.
>
> —Romans 1:19–20 KJV

Lord,

I listen to Your voice and hold fast to You.
For You are my life and the higher power
Who leads me in the way I should go.

Amen

Faith
in the
Storm

By Tamara Boggs

Lying in my bed one night, I was haunted by this Scripture: "If you have faith as a grain of mustard seed, you will say to this mountain, 'Move from here to there,' and it will move" (Matthew 17:20).

A dear missionary friend had died a couple of days earlier after battling cancer. Surely between all of us friends we had enough faith to enable God's healing. Was my friend's cancer a greater obstacle than moving a mountain? I thought he should have been healed—his fervor and dedication to the Lord's work and his compassion and humble spirit were seldom seen in people, even Christians.

I don't feel like asking for anything anymore. How can I have faith that what I ask will be granted when I've followed the Scriptures to the best of my understanding and it just doesn't seem to work? If God doesn't answer my prayers, why does He tell me to ask? My confused thoughts and feelings of frustration were like an inward storm threatening to sink my struggling faith.

I grabbed a tissue and rolled over, wearily whispering a last-ditch-effort prayer. *"God, help me to trust You again."*

In answer to my prayer, God brought a memory of an earlier time when a storm raged around me—a physical storm with wild winds and waters.

I was ten years old. My family and I were owners and crew on the *Sea Angel*, a fifty-foot yacht.

In response to God's leading, my parents had put much of our family's financial resources into building what was going to become a medical missionary boat. We took a maiden voyage around Central America from California to Florida on the unfinished boat. We hoped to complete the work in Florida so it could start on its mission work. But on the way we were hit by a storm.

The hull creaked and shook every time we fell into a valley between the twenty-foot waves. Dishes and pans in the stackable shelves crashed to the floor as the mighty ocean lifted and tossed the yacht like a toy boat in the bathtub. Through the back door I saw sheets of foaming ocean and inky darkness as water towered above the boat. The hum of the twin diesel engines changed pitch and intensity as they fought to keep us on course. Occasionally, they roared a loud crescendo as one of the props came out of the water and we plunged down a particularly high peak.

Even a ten-year-old could tell we were in trouble. I felt frightened.

I left my sleeping bag and held on tightly to whatever was tied down as I fought my way up the stairs to the bridge. There Dad sat braced in the captain's seat with eyes studying the radar screen, occasionally glancing out into the black night.

Dad's face was drawn and filled with concern, but tacked to the wall next to the radar was a tattered 5x7 print of Warner Salman's painting *The Lord My Copilot*. In the picture, a young sailor on a historic sailing ship fights a raging sea with his hands grasping the wheel. Behind him stands a bigger-than-life, translucent figure of Jesus with one hand on the boy's shoulder, the other pointing the way through the stormy night.

Sheets of foaming ocean blotted out the inky darkness as water towered above the boat.

I knew that Jesus was with my dad too. Somehow just seeing him there calmed my fears. I knew that God was in charge and Dad was following His direction.

I made my way back to the living area reassured. Eventually, I went to sleep, although often awakened by the jar of a hard landing. When I awoke the next morning, the engines hummed a steady drone and I knew the storm was over.

While we slept, Dad had fought the storm late into the night, afraid that if he tried to turn back, the oncoming waves would capsize us. Then, at one point he felt the wheel being pulled from his hands. Before he could regain control, we were turned around. Dad was sure God had intervened.

Back in my room, this memory flashed before me. The smell and taste of the salty ocean air was as vivid as my feeling of safety in my father's hands. And with that feeling, that image, that memory, God restored my faith.

The *Sea Angel* did go on to fulfill its ministry.

God would also be in the continuing story of the memories of my missionary friend and in the stories of the people he had brought into God's kingdom. I felt assured that although storms will come in our eternal-life stories, with Jesus as our copilot there is no end.

> Then they cried out to the LORD in their trouble, and he brought them out of their distress. He stilled the storm to a whisper; the waves of the sea were hushed. They were glad when it grew calm, and he guided them to their desired haven.
>
> —Psalm 107:28–30

Lord,

From the rising of the sun to its going down Your name is to be praised. I will not fear the beginning or the end of experience with You.

Amen

Chopped Fruit

By Joyce Meyer

God's goal for our relationships with others is peace. From James 3:18 we learn that harmony with others results from conforming to God's will for us. God knows the healing power of a loving act, and He calls us to minister peace in our homes before He calls us to minister outside of our homes.

When I get up in the morning, sometimes God tells me to do things for Dave that I don't want to do. For example, Dave likes to eat fruit salads. He likes everything all cut up in a bowl. I don't mind taking him an apple, an orange, and a banana, but he wants it all cut up. Then he wants his vitamins and his orange juice and his coffee.

A few years ago we started having a housekeeper come in during the week. She takes care of Dave's fruit salad, vitamins, orange juice, and coffee and she's great. But one day, when it was a holiday, I went downstairs to make coffee in the morning and I was not in the humor to do anything but get my coffee and go back to my room. I wanted to pray and be with God.

That's our problem—we are so spiritual that we just want to "be with God" but don't want to do anything Jesus tells us to do. He said that we need to serve each other. That particular holiday morning the Holy Ghost said, *"Fruit salad."*

That holiday morning the Holy Ghost said, "Fruit salad."

I didn't want to make the fruit salad. I *really* didn't want to make it. I even said, *"I don't want to—I want to go pray."*

Then the Lord said to me, *"Joyce, serving Dave is serving Me."*

So I made the fruit salad.

"And the harvest of righteousness (of conformity to God's will in thought and deed) is [the fruit of the seed] sown in peace by those who work for and make peace [in themselves and in others] . . ." (James 3:18). Peace is something that we sow and then work for in ourselves and in others. The reward is harmony, agreement, and a peaceful mind free from fears, agitating passions, and moral conflicts. Suddenly, in light of God's Word, making fruit salad for Dave was more than an act of conforming to God's will; it was seed that brought peace and joy in my life.

My initial bad attitude reflects the heart of many Christians who will do something in the church for somebody else as their "ministry," but if they do that same thing for someone in their family, they think they're being turned into a slave. But if ministry doesn't work at home, it's not working.

If I'm willing to do something in the church as "my ministry," but won't do it at home, then I have to question myself and find out what is making the difference. Many times at church someone is usually kind enough to tell me how wonderful I was for what I did. They clap and cheer and pat me on the back, when if I do the same thing at home, I may not even get thanked.

How much quicker are we to do something if there's a little something in it for us—a little recognition, a little bit of money, a little bit of promotion, a little bit of favor? I read a statement in a book about love that tore my life up. The author said, "If you want to measure your love life, watch and see how you treat people that can do you no earthly good. If your actions are not coming out of a right heart—if you are doing it to be seen—you have lost your reward. If you are doing it to be well thought of, you have lost your reward." He said, "Do good works in secret; do them to honor God, not to get something for yourself."

God anoints us so we can do something to make somebody else's life better. True happiness is found in the joy you feel after ministering to your spouse and family. Soon, you will want to find other hurting people with whom you can share your gifts, but in most homes today there are enough hurting people in our living rooms who desperately need us.

> Be careful not to do your "acts of righteousness" before men, to be seen by them. If you do, you will have no reward from your Father in heaven.
>
> —Matthew 6:1

Lord,

If I live according to my sinful nature, I will die; but if by Your Spirit I put to death the misdeeds of my body, I will live. Lord, lead me by Your Spirit to live as Your child and to bring life and not death to my relationships with others.

Amen

HE RESTORES OUR SOULS

**He refreshes and restores my life (my self);
He leads me in the paths of righteousness
[uprightness and right standing with Him—
not for my earning it, but] for
His name's sake.**

—Psalm 23:3 AMP

Following the Shepherd restores us to a right relationship with God and others. This righteousness in God leads to freedom from pretense that glorifies God in the eyes of those who watch us. When we follow God, people learn they can trust us and consequently they can trust the God we serve.

Lessons in the paths of righteousness often require risk and vulnerability, but passing the test leads to joy unspeakable as the following stories reveal. Merlin Carother's classic teaching on praising God shows how hopeless situations can be redeemed through God's ability to work all things together for our good.

Sharing, trusting, and giving all demonstrate the Father's heart to our neighbors, friends, and clients. Bruce Davis teaches how integrity blessed his business and showed his employee the blessing of doing the right thing. Susan Gammon found that a small act of kindness brought visible change to her neighbor's life. Bishop Eddie Long's daring act to obey the voice of God proves He knows precisely what we can give and who needs our offering. And Niki Anderson's story of her husband's obedience to tithe proves you can't out give God. Following the Shepherd is the right thing to do.

The Fruit of Obedience

By Cristine Bolley

I asked God if He wanted me to *do* anything before beginning this book.

"*Yes,*" came an unexpected response, "*I want you to walk your dog in the morning before you begin to write.*" Walking sounded easier than writing so I wondered if I was putting words in God's mouth.

The next morning, our golden retriever, Abby, seemed stricken with delight when I reached for her collar and lead. A few minutes into my walk, I asked the Lord, "*Since I am compiling stories about hearing* Your *voice, and answering* Your *requests, do you have an assignment for me?"*

He quickly responded, *"I want you to go to Stan's* house."* Stan's house came immediately into view as I turned the first corner of my walk. We had both served on the homeowner's board a year before, but Stan had resigned from the board without explaining why. God said, *"Tell him you are sorry you offended him and were the reason he withdrew from the board."*

> *If you would come to God more often, He would tell you even more.*

Convinced of my innocence I regretted asking God for an assignment. *"What did I do to offend Stan?"* I argued as I stubbornly walked on past Stan's house. *"If it is really You, tell me specifically what I said that upset him."*

"It was about the shrubs at the neighborhood entrance," He said.

Stan and I had engaged in a lively conversation at that meeting. I had questioned his recommendation to plant photinias because mine had died after a winter freeze. I had challenged other points he made that night too. Besides, committees are supposed to consider all sides of suggestions; yet, admittedly, my method was more rushed than loving that night.

I decided to take Abby to our neighborhood park where I plopped down on a bench.

"Why is it, Lord, that when we talk to each other it seems we're always asking each other for something?"

"Because we don't spend enough time talking together," replied that still, small voice within. *"If you would come to Me more often, I would tell You even more. There will be*

114

moments in the future when there won't be time to ask you twice to do something."

"I'm sorry, Lord." It was all I could think to say on that sunny February day—under that blue sky—on that park bench—as far away from Stan's house as I could get.

Three weeks transpired before I obeyed God. I had stopped taking Abby on morning walks, fearing a forced confrontation if Stan happened to be in his yard. In the meantime, I had told several friends about my encounter with God. To my regret, no one doubted I had heard the voice of God and all agreed that I probably had indeed offended Stan.

To my regret no one doubted I had heard the voice of God.

I knew I wouldn't be able to write this book until I learned the truth about Stan's resignation. Led by both intrigue and my fear of the Lord, I decided to drive to my neighbor's house. It was 11:45 A.M. Reluctant to go at their lunchtime I considered doing errands and stopping on my way back. But a strong "feeling" to go right then compelled me to turn toward his house instead of the neighborhood exit.

Stan was walking to his front door as I neared his home. I waved but he didn't recognize me at first. I pulled up to his curb, hopped out of the car, and extended my hand to shake his, saying, "Hi Stan! I'm Cris. I served on the homeowner's board with you last year. I came to apologize for offending you and causing you to withdraw from service. The president never told me why you left, but I'm sure I was the reason you withdrew and my desire to apologize keeps growing stronger."

"Oh, well," he began, startled by my direct announcement, "you don't need to take the blame. There's always a final straw but many things went into my decision. I'd been on the board for two years and I had just had enough."

"But I'm quite sure *I* was the final straw," I insisted. "And if you will tell me specifically what I did I would like to try to make it right again."

He looked away to gather his thoughts and returned some more excuses, but he mentioned a final straw two more times in his efforts to change the subject.

"How's your family?" he countered.

What a gentleman he is being, I thought as I told him about our daughters' busy volleyball schedule.

"Oh, my daughter coaches volleyball!" he said. We talked about our love for the sport.

Finally, I said, "I have always appreciated all you did for our neighborhood; I remember how you cleaned the fountains before we hired a pool company to maintain them. You brought experience and wisdom to the team, and I enjoyed the energy you added to the meetings. But I *know* I was a catalyst in your resignation and I wish you would tell me what I did so I can thoroughly apologize."

Perhaps he sensed my sincerity, or saw the tears that were forming in my eyes, because he looked at me for a long moment, took a deep breath, and said, "Well, it was about the shrubs at the neighborhood entrance. It was my job as the maintenance director to replace the junipers that had died and I had arranged to plant large red-leafed photinias there. But by the time I talked to Charles, the neighborhood landscape designer, you had already talked to his wife, Mary, about foster hollies. It was a chain-of-command issue, and I just figured if we weren't going to divvy up responsibilities it wasn't worth my time to be on the board."

"Oh, Stan, I forgot about that conversation with Mary. Yes, we had talked of starting a neighborhood garden club and I mentioned that my photinias had died in the winter freeze. I told her I hoped we could find a hardy plant for that location. I haven't even noticed—did the shrubs get replaced?"

"Yeah, there are foster hollies out there just like the one I have dying in my backyard."

My regret was too great. Tears flooded the corners of my eyes as I said, "I am so sorry, Stan. My photinias may have died through my neglect and not because of a winter freeze. I should have let you handle it, but I see I cannot make it up to you now."

His eyes softened as he said, "Ah, some people tell me my German blood makes me too stubborn."

"And I'm told my Irish blood makes trouble for me."

Then he laughed. "My wife is Irish, so we have a grand time together."

A rabbit dashed across his neighbor's lawn then sat calmly looking at us. "That rabbit keeps eating my pansies," he said.

"Oh, that must be what's wrong with my pansies too!" I replied. We talked about the beaver dam that was flooding the creek behind my house, the upcoming neighborhood clean-up day, and various projects that "someone" in the neighborhood ought to look into. As Stan shared ideas that would increase our property values with small cooperative efforts, I realized everyone in our community lost out when he withdrew from the association board.

Somehow our conversation revealed that we were both writers. He shared some of the stories he was compiling about growing up in Germany in 1945. I thought, *Look what I've been missing. What is it to gain a shrub but lose a neighbor?*

Forty minutes must have passed in what seemed like three. I told him to call us if he or his wife ever needed anything since his extended family lived so far away. He thanked me.

As he walked me to the curb he said, "Maybe I will volunteer to serve on the board again next year. I don't have anything going on to keep me from helping."

"I hope you do, Stan. It would be my pleasure to serve on any task team you organize, and I promise not to challenge your leadership."

He grinned and said, "Aw, those punch-outs are part of the process. I'm glad you stopped by, Cris."

Through the apologies, the tears, and the discovery of our common ground I felt forgiven. I was free from the nagging pain in my heart, free of the dread of confrontation, and free to one day return and tell Stan the whole story of how the Lord sent me to his house. Even Abby would be happy that I was free to walk her around the block again.

> If the temper of the ruler rises up against you, do not leave your place [or show a resisting spirit]; for gentleness *and* calmness prevent *or* put a stop to great offenses.
>
> —Ecclesiastes 10:4 AMP

Lord,

Establish my steps and direct me by means of Your Word; let not any offense or injustice have dominion in my life.

Amen

The Power in Praise

By Merlin R. Carothers

J im's father had been an alcoholic for thirty years. All those years Jim's mother, and later Jim and his young wife, had prayed that God would heal him, but with no apparent result. Jim's father refused to admit that he had a problem with alcohol, and stalked out in anger if anyone ever mentioned religion to him.

One day Jim heard me speak about the power that is released when we begin to praise God *for* everything in our lives instead of pleading with Him to change the circumstances that hurt us.

Jim brought home a tape of the meeting and played it over and over again for his friends. Then one day it struck him; he had never tried praising God *for* his father's condition. Excitedly he shared the thought with his wife.

"Honey, let us thank God for Dad's alcoholism and praise Him that the condition is part of His wonderful plan for Dad's life!"

For the rest of that day they gave thanks and praised God for every aspect of the situation, and by evening they felt a new sense of excitement and expectation.

The next day their parents came for the usual Sunday dinner visit. Always before, Jim's father had cut the visit as short as possible, leaving right after dinner. This time, over a cup of coffee, he suddenly asked a pointed question.

"What do you think about this Jesus Revolution?" He turned to Jim. "I saw something about it on the news last night. Is it just a fad, or is something happening to those kids who were hung up on drugs?"

The question led to a lengthy and open discussion about Christianity. The elder couple didn't leave till late in the evening.

Within weeks Jim's father came to admit his drinking problem, turned for help to Jesus Christ, and was completely healed. He now joins the rest of the family in telling others what praising God can do!

"Just think," Jim said to me. "For thirty years we prayed for God to change Dad. We spent only one day praising Him for the situation and look what happened!"

The phrases "Praise the Lord!" or "Thank God!" are used so glibly by many of us that we tend to lose sight of their real meaning.

Praise, according to Webster's dictionary, means to extol, laud, honor, acclaim, express approval. To praise, then, is to give positive affirmation, expressing our approval of something. Giving our approval means that we accept or agree with what we approve of. So to praise God *for* a difficult situation, a sickness or disaster, means literally that we accept and approve of its happening as part of God's plan for our lives.

We can't really praise God without being thankful for the thing we are praising Him for. And we can't really be thankful without being happy about whatever we're thankful for. Praising, then, involves both gratitude and joy.

The fact that we praise *God* and not some unknown fate also means that we are accepting that God is responsible for what is happening. Otherwise it would make little sense thanking *Him* for it.

> And we know that all that happens to us is working for our good if we love God and are fitting into his plans.
>
> —Romans 8:28 TLB

Lord,

I give You thanks for the message of the cross. It is foolishness to those who are perishing, but to us who are being saved it is the power of God.

Amen

Truth
Be
Told

By Bruce A. Davis Sr.

I'm the owner of a small plumbing and heating company. One of my plumbers, who describes himself as "not a religious person," called me from a job he had been on all day. He said I needed to come by right away.

"What's the problem, John?" I asked.

"You'd just better come take a look, boss. I'm stuck and I don't know what to do," he said.

John was in his mid-thirties, and one thing I appreciated about him was his calm and stable nature. But I could tell by his voice that he was upset, so I told him I'd be right over.

As I pulled onto the street where we were working, I saw the big backhoe next to a large pile of dirt in the front yard of our client's house. I stopped at the curb and John met me by my van. John had only been working for me for nine or ten months, but he looked more worried and upset than I'd ever seen him.

"I really blew this one, Bruce," he said. "I've never made a mistake like this in all the time I've been a plumber."

"What in the world happened?" I asked, looking around but seeing nothing obviously wrong.

"What happened is I missed it. I blew it. I told Mrs. Nelson that the broken sewer line was on her side of the property line out here in the front yard and it's not. It's on the city side of the line."

"Oh, I see," I said, as everything became clear.

Mrs. Nelson had called us to fix her sewer line that kept clogging several times a year. John had snaked it for her and cleared it the last two or three times, and she had finally decided to pay to have the line fixed right. John had checked and double-checked, and it had seemed that the bad spot in the line was several feet inside her yard. But now that the seven-foot hole had been dug and the pipe had been opened up to install a clean-out so we could inspect the line, it turned out there was no problem in the Nelson's yard; it was out under the sidewalk.

The city had a problem, not Mrs. Nelson, and we had just spent almost a whole day with two people and a big piece of equipment making a big mess for nothing.

"What do we do now"? John asked. The look on his face told me he knew the gravity and impact this would have on our small company. He was devastated that he had let his client and his company down.

I walked over to the edge of the hole and looked down at the pipe, and as I stood there a peace came over me that I know was supernatural. Instead of being filled with dread or anger or fear, a grace and compassion came over me for John and Mrs. Nelson that was far beyond anything that could have originated in me.

I gazed into the seven-foot hole, but instead of feeling distraught I felt peaceful.

I turned to John and said, "What do we do now, John? That's very simple. We do unto Mrs. Nelson exactly as we would have her do to us and our families if we were in her shoes; we tell her the truth."

"Well," he said sheepishly, "I don't really think she would know the difference if we told her the city needed to come out to double-check things and do a little work on their side of the property line. I mean, well, we have worked here all day and we need to get paid something for what we did. Technically, I didn't guarantee her this excavation would be the only thing needed to get her line working right."

"That may be, John, but from what I remember, we also didn't give her any real expectation that this may happen, and we should have and let her choose the course of action. Mrs. Nelson was counting on us and on our advice, and she took our recommendations. We should have been more careful. We could have called the city to double-check things before we tore up her yard. We didn't, and now we are going to go in there and explain things to her, and tell her the whole truth— and that we will be responsible for what we have done today."

"Man, I'm sorry, Bruce. That's why I called you. I just didn't know what you wanted to do."

"I understand, John, but I want you to know that what I may *want* to do and what we *will* do are two different things here. I'm not doing this because I'm some kind of nice and honest guy, because really I'm not. We are doing this because we run this company according to the teachings of Jesus Christ, and no matter how it may look right now, I know God has allowed this to happen to help shape us into the kind of company and the kind of people He wants us to be. We have a rare opportunity here to act like we believe Jesus taught the truth, and I'm not going to let it pass us by."

My partner and I are Christians, but we are careful not to take advantage of our position, impose our beliefs, or discuss them at any length. But we believe the primary reason we are in business is not to make money but to allow God to use us and what He has given us as vessels through which He can touch the lives of our clients and the people who work with us.

When John saw me connect the casual comments he had heard over the last year by applying them in this life situation, he looked for a moment like he was seeing me for the first time. Our eyes met and locked. We didn't speak, but in those few seconds John really began to know who I was and that, in some mysterious way, his boss had a Boss too.

Then I said, "Come on, man, let's do this."

We turned toward the house and he followed me in to talk to Mrs. Nelson. Needless to say she was surprised that we had misdiagnosed the problem and shocked when I told her this was our mistake and there would be no charge for the work.

We called the city, and they were able to power jet the line clear from the new clean-out we installed by the sidewalk. They said they would change the line in a few weeks when their schedule allowed.

The next day around noon John came in from backfilling and cleaning up at Mrs. Nelson's house. I turned around from my stand-up desk when he tapped lightly on the open door as he came in. He didn't say anything. But he handed me some papers and sat down in one of the chairs by the wall.

In the papers was our invoice for the job marked "No Charge," and clipped to the invoice was a check from Mrs. Nelson for the full $1,800 plus tax.

I looked at the check, and then at John, and back at the check, and then I sat down. Chills and goose bumps covered the back of my neck and arms.

"What happened?" I asked.

John looked straight ahead, gazing with wonder and amazement. "When I went to the door to say good-bye and to give her the yellow copy of the no-charge invoice, she handed me the check. She said she has made honest mistakes in her life too, and she didn't feel right keeping this money. Then she said, 'Thank you' for helping her, and for doing a good job."

Chills and goose bumps covered the back of my neck and arms.

"Wow!" I said. "What did you say?"

"I don't really remember. I was so blown away. I mumbled a bunch of thank-you-very-much stuff—I didn't know what to say."

"So," I said gently and carefully, "what do you think God is up to here?"

And then, John and I talked about this fellow Tradesman and Contractor, Jesus. We talked about His life in Palestine, the truth of His teachings, His great love, His death and resurrection, and the mysterious ways of God in the lives of plumbers.

Though a sinner does evil a hundred times and his days [seemingly] are prolonged [in his wickedness], yet surely I know that it will be well with those who [reverently] fear God, who revere and worship Him, realizing His continual presence.

—Ecclesiastes 8:12

Lord,

I know, my God, that You test the heart and are pleased with integrity. Give me Your wisdom when the opportunity to be tested is before me.

Amen

Let's Share

a
Cab

BY SHARON HANBY-ROBIE

I was feeling frazzled after two days of media interviews for my new book. As I stepped out of the television studio into the pouring rain and rush hour traffic of Chicago, I realized my biggest challenge was ahead of me—to find a cab to the airport in time for my flight home!

Just a few yards beyond me, I spotted another woman on a similar search. I decided to approach her in the hopes of sharing a cab. As God would have it, she too had just left the studio and was also headed to the airport. Fortunately, we soon hailed a cab, threw our luggage into the trunk, and were on our way.

As we began talking, I learned her name was Meredith. She too was an author on tour with a book. *This is exciting*, I thought. *I'll have someone to talk to about my book tour adventure.*

But then I looked at her face. It was full of pain—a pain I recognized. Only divorce can cause that kind of pain. I knew. I had been there.

Instantly, I knew our meeting was a divine appointment—not a time for superficial chitchat, but a moment to minister to a deeply hurting soul.

God said, *"Go on, ask the question."*

I have never been a shy person. Nonetheless, I am amazed at how bold I can be when God says, *"Go!"*

"Are you OK?" I asked.

Her answer was simple. "No."

"What's wrong?" I asked. "Can I help?" I paused and added, "Are you going through a divorce?"

Her eyes welled up with tears.

Seeing her tears caused my mind to flood with memories. I remembered

> *I looked at her and knew. God confirmed it by saying, "Go on, ask the question."*

being in her shoes seven years earlier. Two days after my husband announced he was leaving, I was on a business trip to North Carolina, alone. That morning I awoke feeling numb. I ordered breakfast, and when it arrived, I couldn't eat. Breathing took more effort than I had. I was terrified and had no idea how I would get through the day. But God sent me an angel—a perfect stranger. Her name was Phyllis. Her God-sent help carried me through those three days, and beyond.

Now it was my turn to return God's favor. Meredith was alone in a big city, and she was scared. I told her that I knew how she felt as I related my own tragedy of divorce after twenty years of marriage. I told her I was a Christian and that I believed God ordained this meeting.

"There is a critical turning point in the divorce process where you must accept that it is going to happen whether you want it to or not. The only real choice you have is *how* it happens," I said. "Stop wasting what little energy you have trying to change reality and start taking care of yourself."

Looking into Meredith's face, I worried that I must seem like a freight train coming straight at her. This stranger was peering into and poking her deepest wound.

"I've always been strong," Meredith said. "I've known what to do, taken care of everyone else."

"I understand," I said. "That's how I was. Meredith, go home and sleep. Let your mind and body rest. When you wake, call your most nurturing friend. Tell them what has happened. Let them take over for awhile."

Meredith listened intently.

She had been married for twenty years. She and I were the same age. It's hard to go through divorce, especially at mid-life. Just when you think all is well, all is over—at least that's the way it feels. It's too overwhelming to figure out immediately.

We talked about the mixed signals she was receiving from her husband—signals that sometimes led her to believe he would stay. "Guilt can make people try to soften the blow," I said. "Pay attention to what he does, not what he says. That's where you will find the truth.

"God is ready and waiting to help you get through this— and you will. No matter what else you do, take this opportunity to find the deepest, most intimate relationship you could ever imagine with your Creator."

Our taxi pulled up beside the airport curb. Meredith and I grabbed our bags and parted company. Even though we had exchanged cards, I figured I'd never hear from her again. I breathed a prayer for her as I watched her disappear into the crowd.

A few weeks later I received a letter from Meredith that said, "Thanks for the to-the-airport ministry. I totally, absolutely, without a doubt, believe God is working in my life. I returned from Chicago and spent the next couple of days sleeping. My job is cultivating patience and managing my anxiety."

Three years later while searching for some lost papers, I discovered Meredith's letter. Again, God said, *"Go! Call her."*

Meredith's first words to my unexpected phone call were, "That cab ride changed my life. I will never forget it. How my life has changed since then! I am doing things I never dreamed of attempting before the divorce."

> *Three years later God again said, "Go! Call her."*

It's good to know that God is still in the business of changing lives. Going through a traumatic experience changes us forever. As we are going through it, it may seem we will not be able to survive the pain. But when we allow God to take over, the miracle of healing takes place—and one day we will realize He has actually *erased* the pain! We can know in our heads that we lived that pain, but we will no longer feel it.

And then the next miracle takes place—we are transformed because we already know the "worst" that can happen. Now we are free to be bold and try things we never would have done before because we know we can survive them. Both Meredith and I have gone on to successful new careers many would consider bold. We have opened our hearts, and allowed ourselves to be vulnerable, because we know that God is near, protecting us.

Since you have kept my command to endure patiently,
I will also keep you from the hour of trial that is going
to come upon the whole world to test those who live
on the earth.

—Revelation 3:10

Lord,

*When the day of evil comes, I will put on
the full armor of God, so that I may be
able to stand firm. For Your Truth will
keep me free and Your Righteousness will
be a shield to me.*

Amen

A Still, Small Voice

By Susan Gammon

At the end of a busy summer day, I found refuge from the cares of the world in the midst of my garden. The cool breeze of early evening swirled refreshingly around my body as I leaned on my well-worn hoe.

I spent much of my spare time beautifying the little acre of land that I called my own. Various flowerbeds splashed bright bursts of color in a sea of green. Trees and shrubbery provided the perfect backdrop for a cascading waterfall that flowed into a pond alive with goldfish. I began thanking God for the evidence of His love through the wondrous beauty of His creation.

My gaze shifted to the next-door neighbor's property—a stark contrast. It had been two years since a mower had touched the lawn. Weeds stretched toward the roof of the house. Vines strangled whatever they could wrap themselves around. Trash was strewn around the property. Peeling paint adorned the house. Beer cans littered the driveway. The disarray painted a grim picture of hopelessness and despair.

I felt a nudge to reach out, but I hesitated.

Steve had lived across the hedgerow for several years. We exchanged pleasantries from a distance; neither of us had taken the steps necessary to become acquainted. Although I didn't know him, I had heard rumors of his sad life: divorce, lost children, money concerns, alcoholism. It was easy to see that he'd given up. My prayer of thanksgiving turned to a prayer of intercession.

Steve's sudden appearance startled me. As he opened the hood of his car, I quickly went back to my garden work, hoping that he hadn't noticed me. I felt a little nudge to reach out to this man but I hesitated. *"And say what, God?"*

Although I continued to find excuses, the feeling just wouldn't go away. The realization became clear to me that what I did or said wasn't the issue; that I obey the request of the Spirit was of utmost importance. As I walked toward his yard, I asked God to say it for me—whatever "it" was.

The dialog was a little awkward at first. Then I earnestly asked him how he was doing. The floodgates opened, and he began sharing the details of his troubled life. My heart ached for him, and I sensed that he felt my sincere concern. By the end of our conversation, I felt an overwhelming desire to make a promise, "Steve, I'm going to pray for you."

A grateful smile crept across his face. Hope danced in his eyes as he thanked me.

I turned to go back to my garden, thanking God for the opportunity to reach out in love. I marveled at the wisdom in that still, small voice and the power that comes from obedience to it. As I bent down to reclaim my hoe, my spirit soared. In the distance, the sound of Steve's old, sleepy mower could be heard, growling as if in protest for being awakened after such a long slumber.

But those who hope in the LORD will renew their strength. They will soar on wings like eagles; they will run and not grow weary, they will walk and not be faint.

—Isaiah 40:31

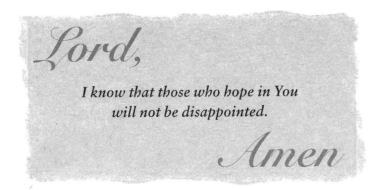

Lord,

*I know that those who hope in You
will not be disappointed.*

Amen

The Storm

By Michael E. Wray

A deafening rattle like thousands of BBs ricocheted on the truck roof and through my brain as I drove in a torrential downpour. The howling wind and rain mirrored the storm raging in my heart.

A short time before Mom had asked me to go to the grocery store to pick up a few things she needed. It was the first time I'd been there since I'd broken up with my girlfriend almost a year earlier.

Walking past the flower display, I remembered how her face lit in delight when I brought her bouquets. We used to walk behind one another through the narrow store aisles pretending we were a two-headed creature. In the health-and-beauty aisle the scent of her peach shampoo wafted past my nose. The special spice potpourri in the cleaning aisle brought back memories of long, after-dinner talks in her living room.

Finishing Mom's shopping became a bittersweet and agonizing trip down memory lane. My heart felt as if a large hand were crushing it. My breathing became labored. I left as soon as possible, but the pain remained, gnawing, growing sharper.

I raged at God, *"Where are You? Why are You letting me suffer? I thought I was over her!"* Heaving and sobbing, I drove slowly down the road, gasping out a prayer for peace and forgiveness.

> *I raged at God. Why was He letting me suffer?*

As quickly as it began, the storm outside stopped. Then a movement at my left caused me to look out the window. A huge owl majestically soared alongside my truck, keeping pace with me. Abruptly, it turned, crossing in front of the truck; its great wingspan extended beyond the fenders as it swooped over, grazing the roof. I slowed to a stop and watched it blend into the night.

That's when God whispered to my heart: *"You ran away from Me, out into the storm, and I followed you. I pulled you out of that relationship before you were crushed, but not before you were wounded. I performed a heart massage to get you going again. You've been sleeping and I am awakening you. I began a work in you and I will finish it."*

The darkness in my heart took wing with the owl that night. Peace wrapped around me like a warm, electric blanket and I sat awed by God's mighty power and grace.

> For the LORD your God is a consuming fire, a jealous God.
>
> —Deuteronomy 4:24

Lord,

I desire to be an instrument for noble purposes, made holy and useful to You and prepared to do any good work. Count me along with those who call on You out of a pure heart.

Amen

Now I Understand

By Kitty Chappell

I liked transcribing, but not full time. When I worked "on-call" status, I could work around my Christian speaking engagements and my writing. But circumstances had changed. When my husband, Jerry, quit his job and started his own business, we lost our benefits. To obtain health insurance, I now worked full time, but I missed the speaking engagements.

I reasoned with the Lord, *"My mind understands, but my heart doesn't. It longs to serve You, Lord. If only there were a key to unlock my door of frustration."*

After finishing a rushed transcription and sending it to the patient's floor, I sighed and noted Betty's* empty desk. It was her day off. I recalled that first morning when she shuffled into the department behind Linda and was introduced. Though she came highly qualified, her appearance was unkempt—sloppy clothes, stringy hair, no makeup. I smiled at her, but my emotions were mixed when she was assigned the desk next to mine. Her appearance wasn't her only unattractive characteristic. Caustic and argumentative, she'd ask me my opinion and then debate my response.

> *I felt trapped and frustrated because I thought I wasn't serving the Lord.*

"I don't know why she asks," I complained to Jerry. "She never agrees with me. Whatever the subject—from vitamins to Christianity—it's always the same. She argues and I pray."

When we typed reports of alcohol-related injuries, Betty always reacted strongly. "Drunks ought to be locked up and the key thrown away." Turning to me, she'd snarl, "Don't you agree?"

"They should be punished, of course, and compelled to undergo rehabilitation before they're allowed to drive again," I said. "It is terrible that innocent people are hurt and killed. However," I added gently, "it's also tragic for drunken drivers. Many are good people who buy into the lie that there are benefits to drinking alcohol—and they live the rest of their lives with guilt for maiming or killing someone."

"Yeah, sure! Try explaining that to the innocent victims!"

Despite Betty's crusty nature, we became friends and enjoyed evening meals together in the cafeteria. I noted a gradual improvement in her appearance and attitude.

Sitting in the cafeteria that evening, I thought, *I'm glad I'm alone tonight.* Then I looked up and saw Betty approaching my table with her tray.

"Don't tell me you've come on your night off just to have dinner with me!" I teased.

"That's right. I'm here to celebrate, and to give you something," she said, tossing a key onto the table.

I picked up the key and looked at her blankly. "New car?"

"Read it," she said, beaming.

"Sobriety, One Year." I shrugged.

"Don't you know what that is?"

"No."

"I received that today for being sober for one year."

"Sober?"

"I'm an alcoholic. I joined Alcoholics Anonymous a year ago after starting to work here. You've been my 'spiritual mentor.' Without you I wouldn't have made it. I'm giving this to you."

"How could I be your spiritual mentor? I didn't even know you were an alcoholic."

"I know. I didn't want someone to just say spiritual things. I wanted someone to care for me as I was. Since my first day here you've accepted me and treated me with loving respect. Even though," she added, "I must have driven you crazy at times."

"I don't understand. How could you learn from me when I didn't know about your problem?"

"Just by talking with you and observing you, I've received all the spiritual counsel I need. You never downgrade anyone and you look for the best in people. I was married to an abusive alcoholic for years. We divorced just before I moved here, and I tried to drown my pain in alcohol. Each time I lambasted drunks I was really berating myself. I hated myself and sought punishment, but you refused to cooperate. You never let me put myself down. You said, 'I wouldn't tolerate anyone else saying bad things about you, nor will I tolerate it from you.'

Your compassionate responses helped me to see that everyone has value—even me. How could I ask for a better spiritual mentor?"

Driving home, something bothered me. *"Lord, I've been scrutinized by Betty for a year and didn't know it,"* I complained. *"I could've blown it at any time, and I wouldn't have known that either! Who else is watching me? This pressure only adds to my frustration of working. I don't understand."*

Later, I understood that I must learn to trust God as much as He trusts me. I had been given the key I had asked for in the midst of my frustration. His trust is a gift—Betty's key was evidence of that gift and was the real reason I was there.

Many are the plans in a man's heart, but it is the LORD's purpose that prevails.

—Proverbs 19:21

Lord,

Thank You for allowing me to show Your power, and to proclaim Your name throughout my world.

Amen

May I Help You?

BY DR. JAMES R. BURKE

I t has never been difficult for me to understand God's protective intervention. As a five year old I fell out of a car on an interstate highway and suffered only scratches. As a seminary student I was driving a car that slid off the highway and rolled over at least twice. I walked away.

While serving as a missionary in Colombia, South America, one of my colleagues related how he had been working on the roof of a new church building when he fell about fifty feet. He landed on an empty five-gallon can that got smashed flat. Although a little sore, he got up and walked away. Of all the places he could have fallen, how is it that he landed on that can?

While I was on a bus, I saw a large sign warning that we were entering a restricted area. People who had not been inoculated against yellow fever were told to stay out of the area. But I spent a week working outside there. A missionary doctor later informed me that if I had been bitten by just one of the malaria-carrying mosquitoes in that infested zone, I would have died.

God chose to intervene by sending a stranger.

In each of these events I knew that God's unseen presence was protecting me. On one particular Saturday, however, God chose to intervene in my life in a different way. He sent a stranger.

One of the churches in Medellin, Colombia, where I was serving as a missionary, developed severe internal problems. The church leaders invited Ramiro Perez, a national leader, to the city to help address the issues.

On the appointed day I was on the way to the airport to pick him up and take him to the meeting. All of a sudden I heard a terrible scraping noise underneath my truck. With some difficulty I managed to stop the vehicle. As I got out of the truck I couldn't help but notice that another vehicle across the road had also broken down. It had been coming from the opposite direction.

When I looked underneath my vehicle I knew I was in trouble. One end of the driveshaft was hanging down on the pavement. *Oh no,* I thought, *of all times for something like this to happen, it had to be on a Saturday afternoon of a three-day weekend.* I walked about a block before I found a place that had a telephone I could use.

"Coy, I need your help," I told one of my friends. "My car's just broken down." I explained to him my location.

"I'll be right there to pick you up," he answered. I then called my wife to let her know what had happened.

Several thoughts occurred to me. I knew that there was no garage in Medellin that was open and could help me because of the three-day weekend. This meant I would have to get someone to push or pull my vehicle back to the apartment. I would also need to figure out a way to get Ramiro Perez from the airport to the meeting. It was apparent that I would not be able to attend the meeting. After making the calls I walked back to the truck.

I had just arrived when a man pulled up behind my vehicle.

"May I help you?" he asked.

"I've got a problem." I stated the obvious.

"Let me take a look!" He crawled underneath the vehicle. "It's the universal joint," he explained. It was at that moment that I remembered that there was an old universal joint on the workbench in the garage of the apartment complex in which I lived. I mentioned this to him.

"Go get it," he said. About that time my missionary friend arrived. I was concerned about leaving my vehicle. Several things had been stolen from it before, and I could imagine coming back to a stripped-down vehicle or perhaps to no vehicle at all.

"I'll watch your vehicle," the stranger said. I had heard those words before with painful consequences when I believed them. Since I had few options, I asked Coy to take me back to the apartment complex. I retrieved the old universal joint and was relieved that my truck was still intact when we got back.

"Here," I told the stranger as I handed him the part. He crawled underneath the vehicle with some of his tools. Since the average earnings of Colombians fall well under two thousand dollars a year, very few Colombians have tools.

"It's fixed," he said after crawling out a few minutes later. He showed me some remnants of the old universal joint.

One of the men who had been working on the vehicle that had broken down across the road approached us. "Our universal joint is out," he said. "I think that I can fix it with the remnants from the one you've just taken off. May I have them?"

"Well, yes," I replied, somewhat bewildered by the sequence of events.

I started my vehicle without any problem. The stranger and I exchanged pleasantries. "I had a feeling that someone needed help," he told me, "that's why I left my home." We then went our separate ways. I picked up Ramiro at the airport and we made the meeting.

The next working day I took my truck to our mechanic. "I need a new universal joint," I explained.

"I'll fix it," he assured me. I returned to pick up the vehicle at the appointed time.

"I didn't do anything to your vehicle," he said. "There's nothing wrong with it."

"But, I've got to go over the mountains to a meeting in Bogota. I've got to have a dependable vehicle." I did not relish the thought of a breakdown on a mountain road.

"There's nothing wrong with the universal joint," the mechanic assured me. "I guarantee it." I made the trip to Bogota without any difficulties. In fact, I never had another problem with the truck after that incident.

Since the encounter with the stranger I've had time to ponder the following:

Two vehicles broke down at the same location with the same problem at approximately the same time.

A mechanic felt the need to take his tools and help someone. He found me in a city of three and a half million people.

An old universal joint fits my vehicle. One might correctly guess that the old universal joint had been taken off my vehicle at a prior time. But how is it possible that the mechanic had the strength and tools necessary to make the repair on the side of the road *by himself*?

How is it possible that the discarded remains of a universal joint could help the other vehicle?

Since that day I have tried to remember what the stranger looked like. Neither my friend Coy nor I can recall his appearance. Was the stranger an angel or merely a human who played an angelic role? One thing is certain. This incident has given new meaning to Hebrews 13:2: "Do not forget to entertain strangers, for by so doing some people have entertained angels without knowing it."

> If you make the Most High your dwelling—even the LORD, who is my refuge—then no harm will befall you, no disaster will come near your tent. For he will command his angels concerning you to guard you in all your ways; they will lift you up in their hands, so that you will not strike your foot against a stone.
>
> —Psalm 91:9–12

Lord,

Because You love me You will rescue me; and protect me, for I have acknowledged Your name. When I call upon You, You always answer me; You are with me in trouble. You deliver me.

Amen

The Lady at the Park

By Therese Marszalek

L ast summer I packed up my three children and headed to a local amusement park for a day of roller coasters, food, and fun. After filling the kids' fists with tickets, I sent them off to the rides and slid onto a bench to enjoy a relaxing break in the morning sun.

Ready to soak in a peaceful moment, I glanced across the park and spotted a man with long stringy hair and torn pants. The undeniable still, small voice of the Holy Spirit instantly spoke, *"I want you to share your testimony with that man."*

I grumbled to the Lord, *"Now wait a minute, Lord, You must be kidding! I can't talk to him; he's too scary looking. Look at his hair and those hippy glasses! Surely You couldn't possibly want me to share my testimony with him. He won't listen. I couldn't have heard You right, Lord!"*

I drew in a deep breath as the tattered man sauntered across the park, heading in my direction. Although there were hundreds of other empty seats available, he plopped down right next to me. Like a perfectly rehearsed scene, the Lord opened our conversation so I could share my testimony with my new friend, Tommy.

Tommy eagerly talked about the rock band he played with at a local bar. A look of surprise fell on his face when I mentioned our church musicians who recently recorded a spiritual rock CD. "I thought churches only sang hymns," he laughed.

"I used to think the same thing about church too," I said. "Church was the last place I wanted to be back then." As we continued to converse, I smelled stale alcohol on his breath.

I told Tommy of my past alcohol abuse. "I thought alcohol could fill the emptiness in my heart. But the emptiness was always there the next morning."

Tommy's round wire-rimmed glasses slid down his nose, revealing eyes of a beautiful man hidden under a hurting heart. He listened intently and nodded in agreement when I shared memories of drinking so much that I had no memory of driving home. His eyes watered when I recalled the guilt I felt driving under the influence of alcohol with my baby in the backseat. "I risked my baby's life," I confessed. It seemed that Tommy was familiar with my past pain.

"One day I was introduced to Jesus and finally discovered the hope I searched for." I paused and smiled, being refreshed at my own testimony. "My life of destruction and hopelessness transformed into a life of abundance and hope through Jesus."

Tommy subtly wiped his eyes, but continued to listen without looking away.

"Do you know Jesus?" I asked Tommy.

He glanced away briefly and then looked back into my eyes. "We've talked," he said, pondering his own words.

His children interrupted us, begging their dad to stay longer, but Tommy was quick to remind them of the bus they had to catch.

"Why don't you visit our church so you can hear some fellow musicians?" I suggested.

> I asked if He knew Jesus. He said, "We've talked."

He took directions to the church and assured me he would try to come to a service. Then he and his children hurried off to the bus stop.

Alone once again, I wondered why God arranged my unexpected meeting with Tommy.

Then I remembered that only hours before my meeting with Tommy, I had prayerfully asked God to use me for His glory. I had petitioned God to bring a lost soul across my path who needed to hear about the love of Jesus. God had a divine purpose for my brief encounter with Tommy.

How thankful I was that God used me in spite of my hesitation and grumbling. I repented and humbly thanked God for allowing me to see Tommy through His eyes—eyes of love.

I still pray for Tommy and regularly glance back at the church entrance expecting him to walk through the door. The day may arrive when Tommy wakes up in a drunken stupor, ready to give up on life. Maybe the Holy Spirit will bring to his remembrance the lady at the park that found hope in Jesus. He may cry out to the heavens as I did long ago. Who knows? God knows.

Unless the LORD had given me help, I would soon have dwelt in the silence of death. When I said, "My foot is slipping," your love, O LORD, supported me.

—Psalm 94:17–18

Lord,

May the words of my thanksgiving for all that You have done be sown as seeds into the lives of others who need Your salvation. Please send someone to reap the harvest of those seeds."

Amen

The Missing Key

By Carol Sallee

My three children were in a grumpy mood. It was a hot summer day with temperatures outside soaring into the hundreds. Inside the house, with no air-conditioning, it wasn't much cooler.

The longer the day went, the more listless and bored my kids became. They hovered around me, wanting me to entertain them. First, they asked me to do a craft project with them. Then, they begged me to play a board game. Then, they wanted a special snack. I was in the middle of a major house-cleaning project and didn't appreciate their constant interruptions.

Although I felt guilty each time I refused their invitations, I continued my work. One item on my never-ending to-do list involved hauling several boxes to our backyard storage shed. I hoped to quickly move these boxes out and proceed with the rest of my chores.

I ran to the kitchen to grab the shed key, but the key had vanished. My irritability grew as I frantically looked for the only key that would unlock the shed. I even prayed out loud in front of my children, "God, I know that You know where the key is. Could You show me where to look?"

As I searched the house in vain, my kids continued to beg for my attention. I felt a nudging in my spirit, *"Carol, you need to stop what you're doing and spend time with your kids. This housework can wait until another day when your children don't need your attention."*

> *God's plans may include a missing key.*

Begrudgingly, I agreed to play their favorite board game with them. When we opened the game, lying right on top was the shed key. I laughed out loud.

"Why are you laughing?" my kids asked.

"God just reminded me that, yes, He did know where the shed key was. He just decided to use it to teach me a little lesson about priorities. Roll the dice!"

> There remains, then, a Sabbath-rest for the people of God; for anyone who enters God's rest also rests from his own work, just as God did from his. Let us, therefore, make every effort to enter that rest, so that no one will fall by following their example of disobedience.
>
> —Hebrews 4:9–11

Lord,

My soul finds rest in You alone;
my salvation comes from You.

Amen

The Holy Tenth

By Niki Anderson

"Honey, I really think we should start tithing." Bob tossed his catechism book on the sofa and paused for my reaction.

"I'm all for it!" I said.

But my agreement belied my fear. Two emotions were at a standoff. I was thrilled with my husband's response to the Sunday school lesson but chilled by the thought of a 10 percent draw on the budget.

Only months before Bob consented to a 20 percent salary cut to place himself in line for a position opening "in the future." I, the family bookkeeper, had already calculated and cut back to accommodate the consequent shortfall. We had just bought our first house and had mortgage payments. The recent arrival of our firstborn added child care to our expenses. There was no margin of cash flow.

For three years I had prayed that Bob would lead us to tithe. Now faced with the answer to my prayer, my heart raced with the facts of mathematics rather than prancing to the cadence of faith.

"Lord!" I prayed. *"I'm so embarrassed by my fear!"* Our budget felt like an enemy. It sneered at me with disbelief!

How like God to arrange a scenario requiring supernatural intervention!

Suddenly I realized God had an agenda for both Bob's faith and mine. This was not a challenge of dollars and cents but of obedience and trust.

Countless times I had been witness to God's provision. As a teenager, as a college student, and as a missionary, I had tithed from my small income. And through all those years had I ever been hungry, deprived of necessities, or delinquent in paying a bill? Never. So here I was—experienced in tithing yet suffering doubts about the outcome.

The next Sunday we dropped our tithe check in the collection plate. By now, Bob and I were united in our act of faith. He smiled when I whispered, "It's almost like an adventure, isn't it!"

At work the following Monday, Bob was called to the Human Resources office. The personnel director asked him to take a seat. "Bob, we need a production supervisor in manufacturing and we'd like you to take the job. Are you interested?"

Since Bob preferred the hands-on work of production over his responsibilities as a buyer, he accepted.

The salary increase accompanying the promotion thrust us beyond the 20 percent cut he'd taken earlier and over-compensated for the 10 percent tithe, resulting in a net income with a surplus. All this only one day after giving a single tithe check!

How quickly and generously God blessed our commitment. Since then, we have never questioned God's claim on the tithe. The holy tenth is wholly His.

> You give God a tenth of your mint, rue and all other kinds of garden herbs, but you neglect justice and the love of God. You should have practiced the latter without leaving the former undone.
>
> —Luke 11:42

Lord,

I will not worry about my life, what I will eat or drink; or about my body and what I will wear. My faith in You is great.

Amen

It Must

Have Been
God

By Bishop Eddie Long,
as told to JoAnn Webster

Bishop Eddie Long spent his usual time with the Lord, bringing to Him the needs of his 13,000-member church, and receiving the Lord's wisdom about the congregation. As he prayed, in his heart he felt the tug of the Holy Spirit telling him that people in the congregation were facing foreclosure. He prayed earnestly for them. As he did, the Lord impressed him even more strongly, *"You take care of it."*

He knew he had saved $40,000 in the bank, and although he didn't know the extent of the needs, he believed God was telling him to give it. Bishop Long continued praying for the congregation's needs as he entered church the next Sunday morning, eager to give them wisdom from God's Word.

As he spoke, he interrupted his sermon when the Holy Spirit nudged him about the foreclosures, and said, "I believe there are people here facing foreclosure and you need a miracle in your life. If that's you, come to the front, I want to pray for you!"

Individuals and couples moved into the aisles and walked slowly to the front of the church.

Bishop Long prayed for them, then said, "Now, what is your need exactly? How much do you need?"

The first individual said, "$2,000."

The second, a couple, said, "$7,000."

On down the row he went, promising to write a check after the service for each one.

He continued with his message and ministered to the rest of the congregation before leaving the platform. As he made his way down, an astonished elder said, "Bishop, that came to a total of $40,000! How much money do you have in the bank?"

"I had $40,000," Bishop Long answered.

"But what if their needs had come to more than that?" the elder asked.

"Then I'd have known it wasn't God."

> Command those who are rich in this present world not
> to be arrogant nor to put their hope in wealth, which is
> so uncertain, but to put their hope in God, who richly
> provides us with everything for our enjoyment.
>
> —1 Timothy 6:17

Lord,

You are the living God, Who made heaven and earth and sea and everything in them. You have shown kindness by giving us rain. You have provided us with plenty of food and filled our hearts with joy.

Amen

WE WILL FEAR NO EVIL

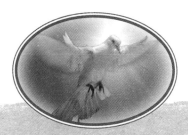

Yes, though I walk through the [deep, sunless] valley of the shadow of death, I will fear or dread no evil, for You are with me; Your rod [to protect] and Your staff [to guide], they comfort me.

—Psalm 23:5 AMP

No one is exempt from walking through valleys of dread at some point in life, but we are not alone if we have put our trust in the Shepherd. He stays with us to protect, guide, and comfort us.

Letting go of our children can be frightening but God promises to hold on to them as He illustrates in my story called "The Kite." Church members who prayed for their property the night before the California earthquake discovered that God is able to keep everything in place even when the earth is violently shaken.

The Shepherd Who made "The Compass" that led John Calhoun to safety is the same one Who led the Mailens through their grief after losing a loved one and Louise Tucker Jones's family through a storm.

Our Shepherd cares about our security, our pets, and our ability to get home. The following stories will build your faith for the next walk you have to take through a sunless valley.

The Kite

By Cristine Bolley

My oldest daughter, Lindsey, was eighteen months old when we bought the rainbow-colored, cellophane kite for her. This kite could catch the slightest breeze and easily took flight without needing to run or have a second person to hold it up. I enjoyed the kite so much that one cloudy morning I decided to try it out in our backyard while Lindsey took a nap.

Soon the kite was soaring in high winds far above the house, dancing with the slightest pull of the string. I wondered how far it could go as I continued to let more and more string loose from the reel. Lindsey had changed my world, bringing focus to playful moments like this which had not been a part of my life before.

In what seemed to only be seconds, the beautiful kite with its fifteen-foot tail was just a tiny speck in the sky.

Higher and higher it danced until a wind current made a threatening tug on the kite string. At first I enjoyed the dance of resistance, but as the wind became stronger I feared the string would break. Not wanting to lose the beautiful kite, I began rewinding the string. Gusty winds fought against my desperate efforts to bring it in and it seemed my rapid reeling was futile.

> *"Parenting is unfair, God. I can't bear the future knowing she will leave me."*

As I wrapped the string around the small rod, I imagined how my little girl would someday tug at the strings that tied her to me so she could break loose and fly freely into the world. The anticipated grief of that moment suddenly filled my heart with pain. These first months of her life had gone by so quickly, and I sensed that eighteen years would come before my heart was prepared to let her go.

I cried, *"Lord, how unfair this act of parenting seems to be! You give me this beautiful child to hold and then require that I teach her to leave me someday. Who knows where the wind might take her? I can't bear the future knowing that she will be gone one day."*

Angry tears blurred my vision of the kite, so I looked at my hands to concentrate on winding the string. I wrapped the string round and round and round the reel as quickly as my arm would move, determined not to lose the kite, yet only progressing fractions of an inch per each frantic twist around the reel.

I sobbed as I fought the wind that day, and the urgency to bring in the kite increased with my dread of losing it.

Somehow, I won the fight. I grabbed the kite when it was finally within reach, and a few days later I gave this painful teacher away.

When Lindsey went off to church camp the summer she turned ten, I remembered the kite. Once again I felt the threatening pull of the wind on the kite when she went on a mission trip to Mexico during her sixth-grade year. Weeks after her return she told me how the van she was assigned to nearly backed off a cliff. Then later, while waiting in the van alone with another girl her age, two teenage boys approached the van and one of them pointed a gun directly at her through the van window.

I remembered the kite as I watched Lindsey go off to camp the summer she was ten.

Uncommon peace covered me as she explained, "I knew the boy was only trying to frighten us. I wasn't afraid and I knew we were going to be all right, so I told Kim to quit crying. That night the friend of the boy with the gun gave his life to the Lord."

I understood the lesson of the invisible wind, that though I couldn't see the Holy Spirit, I could see that He kept her safe and could continue to trust Him to do so. I still didn't delight in letting her loose.

Finally, her eighteenth birthday came, and within weeks it was time for her to go away to college. I wasn't sure how I would endure the day of her departure. Our family held back expressions of our true anxieties inflicted by her transition, and I dreaded watching her pull out of the driveway to begin her first three-hour drive alone to her new life.

She was leaving on a Sunday. I considered letting everyone sleep in and spending a leisurely lunch together before it would be time for her to go. My beloved kite was about to be yanked from my hand, and I wanted time alone to hold onto her a little longer. But somehow I knew that being in church together that day was important.

Praise and worship always brings an awesome presence of the Lord at our church, but prophetic messages from our members are not a standard practice. On this particular day, however, Dr. Ron Meyers, a professor in the School of Theology and Missions at Oral Roberts University, said, "The Lord has a Word of encouragement for us. He spoke to me specifically about four strings: The first is a guitar string. Sometimes our lives are filled with tension, but like a guitar string there is a certain amount of tension that enhances the music that the string plays. God knows how to make the strings in our lives taut enough so that just the right sounds are produced."

Only a few months before I had quit work to begin my stay-at-home-mom-and-write-full-time role, then my husband had been laid off, our daughter was going to college, and our pastor had just resigned from the church. Tension was certainly a part of our lives, but now God was promising to make music with it someday.

Then my full attention returned as Dr. Meyers continued, "The fourth string God wants you to consider is the kite string. You are not to worry when it looks like your kite has been loosed from your hands because God will hold on to the kite string Himself, and He knows how to pull the string so it will soar."

I looked at my husband and three daughters, knowing they were all watching me, knowing that they knew the words about the kite would speak to me, knowing they were watching for my involuntary tears that come when my heart is touched by God, knowing that God had spoken intimately to the deep pain in my heart. I could not fear my daughter's future now—knowing that the Lord had worked eighteen years on this parable for me.

> He who forms the mountains, creates the wind, and reveals his thoughts to man, he who turns dawn to darkness, and treads the high places of the earth—the LORD God Almighty is his name.
>
> —Amos 4:13

Lord,

Thank You that Your love is with those of us who fear You, and Your righteousness is with our children's children.

Amen

$\mathcal{T}$he California $\mathcal{E}$arthquake

BY BILLYE BRIM, ADAPTED FROM
THE BLOOD AND THE GLORY

In early 1993 I began a search that the Lord answered with a revelation of the Blood of the Lamb. When I talked about some of these things privately with my friend, Gloria Copeland, she said, "You need to share this with the body of Christ.". . . It was with a certain amount of fear and trembling that I did so in the fall of '93.

Brenda Steen [wife of Pastor Arland Steen, and co-pastor of Thousand Oaks Christian Fellowship in California] requested [my] tapes. . . . Then the Lord impressed her to preach the series exactly in the order they were [on the tapes]. . . .

She preached on The Blood Line from before the foundation of the world. She emphasized the first

Passover and how they took "a lamb for a house" and drew a [line of lamb's] blood . . . [on the doorframes of their houses,] which stopped the destroyer. She brought in Rahab and the scarlet cord, emphasizing the saving of their possessions. She closed with Jesus' last Passover wherein He disclosed that He was the bread and His Blood was the Blood of the New Covenant which was shed for us [and our protection].

The Holy Spirit surely filled her mouth for she spoke as the oracle of God when she declared quite loudly, "I don't care if we do live in Southern California. I don't care if my house is on top of a fault line. My house will not be destroyed!"

The pastors invited the people to receive Communion "a Lamb for a house."

Pastor Arland said, "Instead of taking it as a congregation, the head of each household led the Communion for their own family, praying a Blood line of protection over each family member and their property."

. . . Brenda Steen sat straight up in bed at 4:31 A.M. only a few hours after dismissal of the Sunday night service. She heard the sound of the powerful quake first. But then she heard another sound. It was the sound of her own voice, "I don't care if we do live in Southern California. *I don't care if my house is on top of a fault line; my house will not be destroyed!*"

Person after person would testify to hearing the same supernatural recording as they gave testimony the following Wednesday night of the miraculous protection they *all* experienced. . . .

Stuart Scholosser awoke to the shaking and rolling that could only mean one thing—earthquake!

"I heard the shouts of the children awaking. Jumping out of bed to get to them, I began to hear loud crashing sounds like things breaking and exploding. My wife joined me as we made our way down the darkened hallway, for the electricity had gone out. We got all the children under the doorways and began praying.

"We began by thanking Jesus that He was here with us, then as the rumbling sounds seemed to get louder we began pleading the Blood [proclaiming God's protection through the power of Jesus' Blood shed for us] first over our home, then ourselves and our neighborhood, then we mentioned wherever the center [of the earthquake] might be. At that point one of the kids said we needed to plead the Blood over my business so we did. . . .

The children reminded Stuart to pray for God's protection for his business.

"Once daylight came we began to assess the damages, finding some broken glass but all else looked OK."

At 9:30 that morning, Stuart left home to try and make his way to his Subway shop located in Northridge. He didn't know then that Northridge sat over the epicenter of the earthquake. He didn't know that a scant mile and a half from his business, one whole floor of the Northridge Meadows Apartments had collapsed killing sixteen people. He didn't know that the University of California at Northridge science building—across from his business—had burned and half the dormitories had been destroyed.

"There was a strange glow in the sky," Stuart recalled, "and parts of the expressway were missing. Police cars directed traffic off the freeway and onto surface streets.

"As I approached the shop I noticed many shattered windows in neighboring businesses. I wanted to just turn around and go home but I continued on. When I pulled into the shopping center where my Subway shop is located I noticed some of my neighbors had damages to their stores. . . I pulled up in front of my store and just sat there staring into the store. Wow! Not one broken window! I then continued into the store to find things had scooted around and things had fallen from the shelves, but besides a few ceiling tiles that had fallen things looked pretty good.

"I began to thank God for the Blood covering that had been prayed over my business and for children that reminded me to pray for the business during the quake.

"I talked to many Subways during the following few days and was amazed to hear of all the damages they had incurred, especially with broken windows and neon lighting, which my store has in excess. But not one tube of neon had cracked.

"God spared my business. But that's not all. The week following we broke all sales records for this location. January is typically our slowest month. We continued to have very strong sales for quite some time afterwards."

> The mountains quake before him and the hills melt away. The earth trembles at his presence, the world and all who live in it. Who can withstand his indignation? Who can endure his fierce anger? His wrath is poured out like fire; the rocks are shattered before him. The LORD is good, a refuge in times of trouble. He cares for those who trust in him.
>
> —Nahum 1:5–7

Lord,

You are a refuge for the oppressed, a
stronghold in times of trouble. Those who
know Your name will trust in You, for You,
Lord, have never forsaken those who
seek You.

Amen

The Compass

By John Calhoun

Not long ago, I was backpacking in the foothills of the national forest near my home. Trying to cram the most into a short weekend, I started out Friday night—with no moon. My two dogs loped out ahead of me, eager for the adventure.

I had a single flashlight as I began to climb the dirt road leading into the forest. I was familiar with the topography and, several days before, had viewed the ridge where I wanted to camp. It looked easy enough to get to—a straightforward, three-quarter-mile hike across a ravine. The ridge overlooked a major canyon—it would be a spectacular scenic prize, eminently worth the effort it took to get there. The east end of the ridge was flat, ideal for placing a tent.

At the place I had to disembark from the road, I stopped to get my bearings. I aligned my compass on the map, getting a reading of 160 degrees to the ridge—roughly south-south-east. I began walking, my eyes flitting back and forth between compass and the dark landscape.

I knew I'd have to go down before coming up. Sure enough, I descended into a ravine, then up the other side, and thought that was it. Then I came to another ravine. And another. I had not seen these on the map—although my map was not the most detailed available. Half an hour later, I stood motionless in the midst of a tangled forest of fallen trees, briars, and vines, wondering where in the world I was. My flashlight was growing dim and I knew that any bear or mountain lion—both of which inhabit these parts—could make quick work of me here.

> *I had followed my compass, but I was not on the ridge.*

By all sensory evidence, I was lost. Intellectually, I knew I had followed the right course, not deviating from my 160-degree azimuth. Then why wasn't I *on the ridge*?

"Lord, help!" I prayed. Into my mind came this Scripture: "Your Word is a lamp to my feet and a light to my path" (Psalm 119:105). *OK*, I thought, *I'll keep following my compass.*

Frustrated and fighting fear, I clawed my way over the trees and up the tangled slope, finally topping out on a small ridge. I wondered if *this* was it—no, it looked too narrow and too well treed, unlike the broad, bare slope I had seen. Against every instinct of mind and body, I resumed my 160-degree course, descending into the next ravine. I knew that if I *had* made a mistake, I was now only compounding it by going farther. I could end up *totally* lost or even at the bottom of some steep cliff.

The next ridge, however, was different—broad and flat, but still treed. Surely I'd gone the required distance by now. Perhaps I had picked a point west of the flat area and now needed to go east. This I did, and quickly emerged into the open. I looked at the map again, finding the green boundary of the trees. I had intersected the ridge *exactly* where I had aimed.

It was 2 A.M. I set up my tent as a quarter-moon rose silently in the east—*now* I could see where I was. Before I could only trust my compass.

Exhausted, I crawled into the tent, followed by my two weary dogs. Lying back on my sleeping bag, I pondered the lessons of this harrowing night. I had followed the true course, but it took me across many hard places—places I had no idea lay between me and my destination. It took a lot of persistence, but the map and compass got me through—again. They never lie. Nor does God.

> Trust in the Lord with all your heart . . . and he will make your paths straight.
>
> —Proverbs 3:5–6

Lord,

**Let Your Word be the unfailing compass
for our lives—trustworthy and true,
despite sensory evidence to the contrary.**

Amen

Shaken

Awake to *Pray*

BY ORAL ROBERTS, ADAPTED BY JAN DARGATZ

Before Oral Roberts married his wife Evelyn, he shared with her the call he felt had been placed by God on his life: "to take God's healing power to his generation." He told her that he knew this call meant that he would be traveling a great deal and that Evelyn would have the burden of raising their children and maintaining their home in his absence.

Evelyn saw her role of wife and mother as being a true helpmate in Oral's ministry, although she never found it easy to say good-bye to him at the airport.

During a crusade more than a thousand miles from home where Oral was preaching and praying for the sick, he was awakened suddenly in the middle of the night as he lay in his hotel room bed. He awoke with a start, as if someone had shaken him awake. Instinctively, he felt a presence in the room, but when he flipped on the light, no one was there. He opened all of the closet doors—no one was there. He went into the bathroom—no one. Suddenly, in his "spiritual ears," he heard the Lord speak to him plainly, *"Your wife and children in Tulsa are in serious danger. Pray!"*

> *"Your wife and children are in serious danger. Pray!"*

Oral immediately realized that an angel of God had awakened him. He fell to his knees, threw his hands and arms over the bed, and prayed as hard as he knew to pray, "Lord, cover every room in the house. Cover my wife, Evelyn, and the children. Protect them and keep them safe." He prayed for some time, with a deep concern and heaviness of spirit, until finally he felt the need to pray lift and a calm enter his spirit.

When Oral returned home, he learned from Evelyn what had happened that night. After she and the children had gone to bed, she had heard a loud noise downstairs at the outside door that opened into the dining room. Someone was rattling the door trying to get in. She was so frightened she began to shake, but she couldn't move. She felt paralyzed by her fear— too afraid to get out of bed or even to turn on the light and call the police. In spite of her fear, her faith began to rise. She prayed, *"Lord, help us! And let Oral know we're in trouble so he'll pray too."*

In a few minutes the rattling stopped. The would-be intruder left and never came back.

Oral asked Evelyn the time of night she had heard the noise. It was the exact hour that Oral had been awakened and told to pray.

Out of that experience, Oral began to preach with renewed conviction one of the hallmark messages of his ministry: "There is no distance in prayer." Because of the Holy Spirit, prayer is never limited by the physical laws of time and space. A "prayer cover" can always be raised over the life of a loved one, near or far.

Jesus praying to the Father said, "My prayer is not that you take them out of the world but that you protect them from the evil one."

—John 17:15

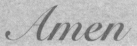

Lord,

I seek Your wisdom, Your understanding; I remember Your words and will not swerve from them. Your wisdom protects me and watches over me.

Amen

$\mathcal{I}$ Couldn't $\mathcal{P}$ray

BY KAREN HARDIN

Christian gatherings outside the confines of the government-established Three-Self Church in China are forbidden. Yet the number of believers in China is growing daily. One of the greatest difficulties for these faithful Christians is how and where to meet together. In most instances meetings are moved from home to home to avoid detection.

One night we hosted a meeting in our home. A muffled knock at the door signaled the beginning of their arrival. They came in small groups of two or three at a time, quietly entering our home to the greetings of their fellow believers.

My husband and I had been married only three weeks when we moved to China. According to the government, we were there as English teachers working on a university campus. According to our hearts, we were missionaries.

There was a hushed expectation as the believers talked among themselves. This was not our regular weekly meeting to study the Word. The Chinese believers had requested a special gathering, stressing that it was urgent. Unable to discuss anything further over the public phone lines, we agreed to a time, curious as to the special need. I scanned the faces of those seated around our living room—faces my husband and I had come to love. Most were new believers, young in their faith. Some were university students, some teachers, some factory workers, but all had a growing hunger for the Lord.

Elizabeth had throat cancer, a death sentence in China.

We noticed one young girl we didn't recognize; although it was evident the rest of the believers knew her. It turned out she was the source of the urgent request for the meeting. Her name was Elizabeth and she had just been diagnosed with cancer.

Elizabeth was in her early twenties and was a nurse at a local hospital. What at first had seemed to be a chronic sore throat was finally diagnosed as throat cancer. The diagnosis of cancer in America emits great fear, but in China it is an almost certain death sentence due to lack of medical knowledge and equipment. The believers had brought Elizabeth to us for prayer.

We briefly discussed the situation and then shared Scripture in God's Word regarding healing. As we were about to pray for Elizabeth, I sensed in my spirit that we weren't supposed to. Surprised, I continued to seek His guidance regarding this young woman. It was evident that Elizabeth and the group of believers not only understood but also had faith for healing, so why couldn't I pray? Their eyes expectant, they looked to us to lead. And then I knew. *We* weren't to pray for Elizabeth. *They* were.

Uncertainty clouded their faces as we encouraged them to lay hands on Elizabeth and lead the prayer themselves. It was obvious this wasn't what they had hoped for. They had believed that we would help their friend. But God was pushing them out of the nest in which they had grown comfortable.

After much encouragement they circled their friend and began praying. Tentatively at first but with growing strength and faith, they prayed.

I'll never forget that night. After half an hour of intercession for this young woman, the prayer quietly closed, and gradually our Chinese friends left in the same small groups in which they had come. Elizabeth was scheduled for surgery soon after and seemed to make a miraculous recovery. However, a couple of months later the pain returned full force. It seemed the cancer was back. The believers were discouraged. They had prayed fervently for her healing, how could the cancer return?

Elizabeth went back for additional surgery. The doctors did discover something in Elizabeth's throat, but it wasn't cancer. During the original surgery the doctor had inadvertently left a surgical sponge inside her throat, which was now causing infection as the body reacted to the foreign substance. Once it was removed Elizabeth healed quickly and experienced no further complications. Now ten years later, she has had no recurrences of cancer.

What had been a life-threatening situation for one woman became a tool of growth and faith for all the believers as they realized that *their* prayers were effective and God heals even today.

He said, . . . I am the LORD, who heals you."

—Exodus 15:26

I praise You and remember the many wonders You have done. You have heard my cry and given me a firm place to stand. Let me always put my trust in You.

Amen

Anthony's Song

By Vonda Mailen

We walked through a dark valley the night my baby grandson, Anthony, went to be with Jesus.

My son and his wife had struggled through a difficult pregnancy, which had placed her and the baby in a "high risk delivery" situation. Doctors were forced to surgically deliver the baby before his due date.

The little boy struggled on the machines for three days, and then the medical staff recommended that the baby be removed from life support. The doctors' best efforts were not working. The shunt had failed.

Painfully, my son and daughter-in-law made the decision to pull the life support off and wait to see if the baby would survive. We were told we could be with

Anthony before he was removed from the machines. As we looked upon his sweetness, the nurse approached and said that we should talk to him.

I stepped closer and spoke, "Anthony, Jesus loves you very, very much! And we all love you too."

Then something unexpected happened. He opened his eyes and looked at us. His little face was radiant.

The nurse began to talk excitedly saying that he shouldn't have been able to do that because he was heavily sedated.

But he did and we knew that he had heard our words and responded. Shortly thereafter, he was removed from life support. Anthony's father and mother asked the chaplain to baptize him. They placed him in his mother's arms. While my son stood bravely beside his wife, their precious little boy went to sleep so he could wake up in the arms of Jesus.

I kept crying, praying, and talking with the Lord. *"I know some day I'll understand but right now I feel so much pain and loss. I believe Your promises and I know my little grandson is with You."*

Within hours, Jesus gave me a vision for healing. I was standing and looking at a long, winding road in the most beautiful place I had ever seen. It led upward to a glowing and glistening city that shimmered with the radiance of the sun. The sky was an endless blue of such depth and tranquility that it immediately engulfed me with inner calmness.

There were two people on this road. The little figure was the most beautiful, perfect child with dark, curly hair and an absolutely beautiful smile on his little round face. He was hanging on tightly to the hand of the tall, strong-looking man. As I looked closer I knew in my spirit that the child was Anthony and he was with Jesus.

Jesus looked straight at me. His eyes penetrated my aching soul and suddenly I was free of pain. My tears flowed and flowed, but they were now tears of gratitude because I was being shown where Anthony was going and Who was taking him there.

And out of my tears flowed words, like a song, that I wrote down and later shared with all around me. I call those words "Anthony's Song."

When calamity comes, the wicked are brought down,
but even in death the righteous have a refuge.

—Proverbs 14:32

Lord,

I am not ashamed to testify of You. Even in my suffering I believe in Your power to save us and call us to a holy life.

Amen

A Safe Harbor

BY LOUISE TUCKER JONES

I t was our third day at the beach, but the tranquillity I sought from the gulf shores eluded me. I walked barefoot, squishing through wet sand while water lapped at my ankles. The salty sea breeze cooled my face, but I cried inwardly, *"Where is the peace I came for, Lord?"*

Later I lay in the shade of an umbrella and watched my husband and son ride the waves in an inflatable boat. Jay, our youngest son, has Down's syndrome. He loves the ocean and was as happy as I had ever seen him. Soon he was running across the sand, pulling his boat behind him. He collapsed beside me for all of sixty seconds, and then grabbed his shovel and pail and began digging in the sand.

This was my cue. Dad handled the waves; Mom built the sand castles.

After a feeble attempt at castle turrets, we built a bridge, shaped a turtle, and then switched to nondescript objects as Jay scampered back and forth to the water's edge to refill his bucket with water. We played and laughed and splattered each other with wet sand. Jay was such a joy, and he loved the beach as much as I did.

The crashing waves, the graceful gliding seagulls, the blue skies overhead all spoke of God's majesty. Here I had always found serenity. But not this trip.

My worries wouldn't fade. In three days we would be in Houston, facing Jay's medical prognosis. Would the doctor recommend open-heart surgery despite the extreme risk? Would he say, "I'm sorry, there's nothing we can do," and give Jay just a few more years? We had been told that Jay would not outlive his teens, and he was thirteen already.

> *Would the doctors recommend surgery or say there was nothing they could do?*

"*Oh, Father,*" I prayed at night when Carl and Jay were asleep, "*give me peace. I have joy. Being here, watching Jay play gives me such pleasure, but deep in my soul, I have no peace. My fears are so great, Lord. I can't seem to release them.*" My cheeks were damp with tears when I finally fell asleep.

After days of beseeching, I gave up. It seemed relief from my inner turmoil wouldn't come, not even here.

Near the end of our stay, we made reservations for a sunset cruise. It was a big step for me; I'm not comfortable with boats and, especially, water. I can't swim! I know how to float on my stomach, but that's not much of a survival technique. The woman we bought tickets from assured me the boat had life preservers and that the ride would be smooth. So, the world's greatest coward headed to sea—near nightfall at that.

My husband was excited about the excursion. We were first in line and got the sought-after seats on the top deck. My heart pounded as I took deep breaths to relax.

The trip started easily enough. The captain narrated and Carl took pictures as we cruised through the harbor. I watched the water uneasily, seeing sharks where everyone else saw dolphins.

But by the time the last rays of sun faded, I had calmed down and was glad I came. By then, we were headed for the channel. Suddenly, the boat began to jolt and the waves grew choppy. What was happening? Up and down, up and down, we went.

People standing on the bow screamed as water sprayed them. Jay slipped onto my lap. I circled my arms tight around him, wondering what I was doing on a boat in the gulf waters at night with my child when I couldn't even swim.

What would I do if the boat wrecked? What if—I was silently reprimanding myself when a woman walked over to me.

"Don't watch the water and you won't get seasick," she said matter-of-factly.

Seasick? Right now I was more concerned about my life. I looked up at her.

"Just watch that light," she said, pointing in the distance. "Don't look at the water moving below. Keep your eyes on a stationary object."

For the next half hour I concentrated on the harbor lights and reminded Jay to do the same. Finally, we cruised into calmer water and into a safe harbor. I came ashore a little more experienced and a lot wiser. Out on those choppy waves, God had used a stranger to speak His message to me.

I had been concentrating on the turbulent sea in my life. I had missed seeing God as my stationary object, my light on the harbor. Watching Him, instead of the waves, would lead us to safety, no matter how deep and dangerous the waters.

Years have passed since that night on the choppy gulf waters. Jay is now twenty-five years old. He still has progressive heart disease but he has astounded the medical community. I also still find myself watching those turbulent waves of stress and worry at times. Then God reminds me that He is my peace, my rock, my shelter—my safe harbor in every storm.

> *"Don't look at the waves; look at that light on shore."*

Thus God, determining to show more abundantly to the heirs of promise the immutability of His counsel, confirmed it by an oath, that by two immutable things, in which it is impossible for God to lie, we might have strong consolation, who have fled for refuge to lay hold of the hope set before us. This hope we have as an anchor of the soul, both sure and steadfast.

—Hebrews 6:17–19 NKJV

Lord,

I will proclaim Your name and praise Your greatness! You are the Rock. You are a faithful God Who does no wrong, You are upright and just, and I will keep my eyes upon You.

Amen

Free

as a
Wildflower

By Nanette Thorsen-Snipes

For the first time in my married life, I had the opportunity to spend two weeks at a mountain retreat honing my writing skills. As I left my husband and children behind, I knew I was going to a place where my thoughts could soar as free as an eagle.

In my newfound paradise, I never dreamed I would come face-to-face with fear. Lugging my computer from the car, I discovered my cabin at the Hambidge Center in north Georgia was on a deserted stretch of road almost hidden by tall weeds and unkempt bushes.

As a resident of the center, I was encouraged to spend time in the isolated natural surroundings—to develop what Mary Hambidge, who founded the retreat, envisioned as a creative life for artists based on nature.

That first evening on the screened porch, I watched the sun ball sink behind the myriad trees leaving in its wake a heady splash of bright orange.

Scratching noises in the attic awoke me. My heart pounded.

At my desk, I arranged a stack of writing books, a thesaurus, and a writer's market guide next to my computer. Sitting in front of the screen, I began to write. The first hour went well, but as the evening wore on, fear niggled at my brain. Something from my past was triggered by my being alone and vulnerable.

After eating a bowl of soup with oyster crackers, I tried to relax on several pillows in front of the fireplace. There was a definite chill in the air, not from the late summer night, but from haunting memories several years before when my former husband had threatened my life. I shook the irrational fear away. A couple of hours later I fell asleep.

A noise in the attic roused me. Startled, I sat up. My heart began to race. I strained to hear the noise again. Memories of that fear when my first husband dogged my steps for months rose again. I put a hand to my chest to quiet my racing heart.

My breathing quickened as I walked to the bottom of the stairs and looked up the skinny stairway. It was odd, but that was the first time I noticed the door at the top. What was behind it? My imagination went into overdrive. With grim

resolve, I had to know what the noise was before I could fall asleep again. Easing up one narrow step at a time, I felt a chill trace my spine.

Then, with my hand shaking, I turned the knob. Locked. I listened intently, trying to figure out the scratching sound coming from inside. Finally, I decided it was mice playing a game of chase across the floor. Of course, it was only mice.

Still shaken, I walked downstairs and made a cup of cocoa to settle my nerves. Whispering a prayer of thanks, I sipped the hot drink, read a chapter of a novel, and lay down to sleep. When I awoke exhausted, I wondered if I could face another night. Deep down, I wondered if I could continue my stay at the retreat.

As sunlight streamed through the pine trees, there was a welcome sense of peace in the warmth filtering through the window. Pouring a cup of coffee, I meandered down a well-worn path to the nearby woods. With sun kissing the wild-flowers and a lone frog hopping beneath a flowering bush, I made my way through some underbrush and down a hillside to a waterfall.

Warming my hands on my cup as I walked, I breathed in the earthy scents around me. Reaching the bottom of the hill, I sat on a moss-covered rock, soaking in God's peace as I watched the water churn over river rocks.

When I returned to the cabin, I flung open the door flooding the room with sunlight much like my soul had been flooded with God's presence. I stayed two weeks, gaining a renewed sense of peace as I wrote poetry and fiction.

One moonlit night after a group dinner toward the end of the retreat, I walked with other artists toward my cabin. The brightness of the evening made me look up. My breath caught in my throat as I saw a full moon grace the top of the mountain like a crown. The moon hung shimmering, its brilliance lacing the night clouds. In that moment I realized that through my trust in God I had finally broken free of my fear, free as the breeze that rifled my hair, free as a wildflower dancing in the wind.

In my anguish I cried to the LORD, and he answered by setting me free.

—Psalm 118:5

Lord,

You are my refuge and strength, an ever-present help in trouble. Therefore I will not fear.

Amen

My Dog, Thrasher

By Annetta P. Lee

I'm a dog lover, and very picky about the diet of my thirteen-year-old mixed breed. Unfortunately, my husband thinks that all dogs should be able to gnaw on a bone—any bone as long as it once had meat wrapped around it.

Thrasher is a large, black, fluffy dog—part chow. Even at his age, he's affectionate and playful with my husband and me. Whenever I go outside, he's waiting for me to give him his warm embrace or go for a vigorous walk through the neighborhood.

One evening after arriving home from work, I noticed that Thrasher was a little timid about approaching me. His food and water dish were virtually untouched. After a few moments, however, he settled close to me nuzzling my hand for his playful rub.

Moved by his initial reluctance, I laid my hand on his head and began to pray. The next day, though Thrasher still sauntered lovingly to my side, he wasn't himself. When I noticed a revolting froth around his mouth, I became overwhelmed with concern, thinking that he may have been bitten by something. I pictured my sick dog with rabies. As apprehensive as I was about staying in the backyard with him, I couldn't imagine how to get him to the vet. I began to pray, and got the impression that I was to look into Thrasher's mouth.

Well, that certainly couldn't be the Lord, I thought. Thrasher could literally tear my arm off, if he wasn't himself. Besides, the Lord wouldn't waste His words on something so irrelevant as a pet.

I got a strong impression that I should look in his mouth, but I didn't do it.

I mentioned the problem to my husband, Kenneth, and said we needed to get Thrasher to the vet if he wasn't better by morning.

Before I went to bed, I prayed that Thrasher would be healed by morning. Then I opened my Bible and turned to Proverbs, as I often do before bed. I came upon Proverbs 12:10: "A righteous man regardeth the life of his beast: but the tender mercies of the wicked are cruel" (KJV).

The impression to go look in Thrasher's mouth came back so strong that I couldn't deny it. Praying for God's protection, I got Kenneth to bring Thrasher inside. Thrasher's eyes lit up as he moved close to my side, just as loving as ever.

After cleaning his mouth with a cloth, I looked inside and found a large bone lodged between his jaw and back teeth that had prevented him from opening or closing his mouth. Kenneth had inadvertently given Thrasher the bone from a pork roast several days earlier. My husband got the pliers and dislodged the culprit. I broke into tears of joy and praise at the compassion and love of God. God really does care about the things that concern us.

> In his hand is the life of every creature and the breath of all mankind.

—Job 12:10

Lord,

If I call out for insight and cry aloud for understanding, then I will understand the fear of the Lord and find the knowledge of God.

Amen

Angels
on
I-40

BY SUE ANN BROWN

The car lost momentum and gradually slowed as I carefully maneuvered it onto the shoulder of the highway.

Desperate, I pushed the accelerator to the floor. The motor roared, but the car didn't move. *OK,* I said to myself, *adjust the gearshift and try it again.* Nothing. Second gear—nothing. Low—nothing. Reverse—nothing.

"Please, God, just give me any gear," I prayed as I repeated the gear shifting process. My fears were confirmed. I had a perfect engine and a dead transmission.

"Well, that's it," I said as I leaned my head back against the seat.

"What, Mom?" my fourteen-year-old son asked.

Sighing, I turned to find six eyes staring at me from three frightened faces. My sons knew we were in trouble.

"There's something wrong with the transmission," I said. "We'll find a station and see if we can get it fixed."

"You mean *walk*?" the fourteen-year-old exclaimed.

I nodded, afraid my voice would crack if I spoke. It was Sunday afternoon, the Fourth of July, and 95 degrees. Our car had just stranded us on Interstate 40, approximately 140 miles west of Nashville, Tennessee,

> *We were stranded 480 miles from home.*

and 480 miles east of home. My three sons and I had been on our way back to Tulsa after a week's vacation in Nashville.

The station wagon rocked as semitrailers loaded with freight whipped past. I dreaded getting my boys out of the car and walking down that narrow shoulder for who knew how long before we found help.

"OK, boys, there must be a gas station not too far from here. We'll be fine," I said, with more assurance than I felt. "Let's pray before we get out of the car and ask God to help us and protect us."

Huddling together, we held hands and asked the Lord to be with us in our time of need, to protect us from injury, and to send someone with whom we could feel safe to help us.

"Mom, we're not going to die here, are we?" my eight-year-old asked. His solemn eyes and quivering chin melted my heart.

"No way!" I replied. "God has angels—even on I-40. Now, everybody out." I reached across his lap and opened the passenger door.

"Don't worry, Mom. We won't have to walk far," my God-confident, twelve-year-old son said. "God says we should ask for what we want and He will answer. We asked. He'll send help."

I smiled as I marveled at how simple things are when we are twelve and don't have battle scars from life's wars and worry. Placing myself between my sons and the solid stream of interstate traffic, I started my little group down the shoulder of the road. I didn't want to think about how far it was until the next exit.

> *My twelve-year-old prophet was sure we would be rescued.*

We hadn't gone more than twenty yards when a car pulled over in front of us. A tall, lanky man with a smile all over his face crawled out of the car.

"Y'all look like ya need some help," he said in that friendly Tennessee drawl we had heard so often over the past week. "We can give y'all a ride." The two women with him motioned to us, making room in the backseat.

"See, Mom, I knew God would send someone fast," my twelve-year-old prophet said as he strode ahead. "Come on."

I surveyed the trio in the car and immediately felt the peace of God about these heaven-sent rescuers. They had rearranged themselves and their belongings, leaving plenty of space for the four of us.

As he pulled back onto the highway, our driver explained that he had a friend who worked at a truck stop a few miles ahead who was a good mechanic. It would be a good place to get help and a safe place to wait, he assured me.

A direct answer to my most fervent prayer, I thought. *"Thank You, Lord."*

We drove several miles before we finally came to the truck stop. The young man had been right. The people who worked there were kind. While we waited for the tow truck to pick up the car and bring it in, my sons enjoyed French fries and soft drinks on the house, thanks to the waitress in the restaurant. After the mechanics declared the transmission officially dead, the truck stop manager graciously offered to store my car free of charge until I could make arrangements to have it fixed.

It had been a stressful day, and we all needed rest. Thankfully, our new friends at the truck stop gave us a ride to a nearby hotel. While the boys cooled off and washed all their cares away in the hotel swimming pool, I made arrangements for a rental car to take us to Tulsa.

The next morning, the world looked brighter, and the trip home was a breeze. The boys cheered as we crossed first into Arkansas and then into Oklahoma. Every state line meant we were getting closer! We reached home just before dark. Home had never looked so good. Standing in our driveway, we could finally laugh about the events of the past two days.

Many years have passed since that vacation, and many trials have come and gone. But my sons and I have never forgotten the lesson learned on the side of that highway: God answers fervent prayer. He will always be with us in times of trouble—providing protection, sending help, and meeting our every need.

God does surround us with angels—even on Interstate 40.

Even to your old age and gray hairs I am he, I am he who will sustain you. I have made you and I will carry you; I will sustain you and I will rescue you.

—Isaiah 46:4

Lord,

I will not fear, for You are with me; I will not be dismayed, for You are my God. You will strengthen me and help me; You will uphold me with Your righteous right hand.

Amen

My Important *Writing* *A*ssignment

By JoAnn R. Wray

On September 12, 2000, my husband, Roger, and I returned home from a meeting to learn that his only sister, just forty-five years old, had died in a terrible automobile crash. We grieved especially because she'd run long and hard from Jesus Christ for years. Where did she stand at that moment?

My husband withheld his grief until he saw his baby sister in the casket. Then he burst into sobs, hugging me tightly. Several times he touched her hand, he told me later, to remind himself she wasn't really there, only an empty shell.

My thoughts were riveted with desire to know if she'd truly accepted Christ. I studied the people gathered. Many, deeply shocked over this tragedy, didn't know Christ. When the pastor delivered his sermon, it was a feeble attempt to comfort, never having met her or talked with her. Where *was* God in all this, I wondered?

After returning home, I talked with a friend and she asked, "Isn't she the one God had you send that letter to last year?"

"Letter?" I thought back. Then I remembered. *How could I forget?*

> *For weeks I tried to ignore, evade, and whine my way out of writing that letter.*

For weeks I'd whined and evaded what I knew God wanted me to do—send a pointed, straightforward letter to Roger's sister and ask her to choose Jesus. He wanted to win her heart to His.

Oh, how I tried *not* to write that letter. I didn't want to be accused of causing family strife or offending her. *She's never listened to me before, God, why would she now?*

Patiently, He listened to all my fears, gripes, and recitations of her bad choices. In the end it didn't matter. All that mattered to God was that she come to Him. Would I write the letter or not?

Finally, I sat down late one night to write it. First, I prayed, *"Heavenly Father, please forgive me for not obeying immediately. Please let it not be too late. Give me Your words, not my own. Let this come straight from Your heart."*

Four, single-spaced pages later, shaking and weeping every line, I finished. A week passed before I reread it. When I did,

I wept all over again. Still I didn't mail it. More days passed. Finally, I asked Roger to read it. He cried all the way through, too, then said, "You *are* mailing this, aren't you?" I hesitated, but at least I put it in an envelope, adding a stamp.

Two days later I read it to my friend on the phone and asked her opinion. She said, "JoAnn. It's important—mail it *now*." Then we prayed for my sister-in-law.

The next day Roger and I prayed over the letter, carried it to the mailbox, and released it.

I won't know until eternity the full effect of that letter. She didn't call in anger—she never said anything at all. That doesn't really matter.

God told me to write it and mail it as a love letter from Him. Across the top of the first page were these words: "Come Home, My Daughter says the Lord." Toward the end I wrote this: "I don't expect you to like this letter and what it says. But I can tell you I've written it in love. I've tried my best to communicate God's heart in these words."

When I think how I nearly did not obey God, nearly failed to write or send that letter, I shudder. God gave me the greatest writing assignment I've had to date, and I almost blew it. We've since learned that Roger's sister quietly moved toward God and came closer to Him shortly after my letter arrived. I'll only know how close when I reach heaven.

From this day on, I will always obey the Lord and write what He instructs. Obedience is better than sacrifice. Every day I see the joy in it more. A copy of the letter I almost didn't write hangs near my computer to remind me.

However, I consider my life worth nothing to me, if only I may finish the race and complete the task the

Lord Jesus has given me—the task of testifying to the gospel of God's grace.

—Acts 20:24

Lord,

I pray that whenever I open my mouth, words may be given me so that I will fearlessly make known the mystery of the gospel, for which I am an ambassador.

Amen

She Will Live
and
Not Die!

BY EDWIN LOUIS COLE,
AS TOLD TO JOANN WEBSTER

The Board of Directors for the Christian Men's Network assembled in the conference room of the International Headquarters, eager to complete the business at hand. Their president, Edwin Louis Cole, was attending another pressing matter and would join them later. Interrupting their meeting, a call suddenly rang through with an emergency for one of the directors.

Jim took the call only to discover that his pregnant daughter was seriously ill. While she was trying to deliver twins, toxemia threatened her life and the

207

lives of her infants. The directors watched Jim's face drain of color as he listened to the report. He dropped the telephone, reported what happened, and the entire group spontaneously broke into prayer as he quickly left for the hospital.

Meanwhile, Dr. Cole had completed his business and was driving toward the meeting when suddenly the prompting of the Holy Spirit rose within him and he began to pray earnestly, fervently, and loudly. The words came out, "She will live, she will not die!" Relentlessly, the words welled up in him and he said them repeatedly until he was almost shouting.

Bursting through the doors of the conference room, Dr. Cole didn't even notice the prayer meeting going on, but blurted out, "She will live, she will not die!"

The directors stopped, stunned. Then they began to rejoice. Each wondered if the other had slipped out of the room to call Dr. Cole, but no one said a word.

Later, Jim called the directors from the hospital to tell them his daughter had made a sudden change and his new grandchildren, twin boys, had been born. The entire room of people erupted in praise to the Lord. Dr. Cole couldn't understand their enthusiasm about the somewhat mundane experience of childbirth.

"Don't you know?" one person asked him.

"Know what?" Dr. Cole said.

"Your prayers were answered. Jim's daughter was at the point of death!"

Dr. Cole looked blank. He blinked a few times before he realized the significance of his own prayers. He never knew for whom he was praying, only that he needed to pray. God performed the miracle as he prayed in obedience to the Holy Spirit's prompt.

And he who searches our hearts knows the mind of the Spirit, because the Spirit intercedes for the saints in accordance with God's will.

—Romans 8:27

Lord,

I will not speak of my own accord, but I will speak what You command me to say.

Amen

HE ANOINTS US

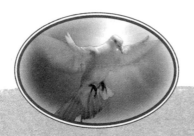

You prepare a table before me in the
presence of my enemies. You anoint my head
with oil; my [brimming] cup runs over.

—**Psalm 23:5** AMP

The image of a table before us that has been prepared by our Shepherd is an amazing concept. In most kingdoms on earth the people prepare a table for the king, but our King sets us before the people of the world and says, "Look at my flock. Look at all that I want to give them. Won't you join us at my table?"

Evangelist T. L. Osborn discovered that the gospel of Jesus Christ had to be better than the message of other world religions if he was to have an impact on the mission field. He sought God and found that in God's presence is the power and anointing of the Holy Spirit to loose people from their sins and sicknesses. After Jesus visited the Osborn's house, a revival swept through their ministry and into the world.

Our needs vary from miraculous to minute but God is able to respond with His anointing to satisfy them all. My brother-in-law, Michael Bolley, tells of God's physical provision during his missionary trip to Colombia, and Koshy Muthalaly shows how God provided emotional comfort for his son on Christmas morning.

When the Norwoods needed a building for their school, when Troy Sledge's mission team needed food and more toys, when Dan needed healing for his swollen eye and a new believer needed help choosing a Bible, God prepared blessings for all of them that were more than enough.

When Jesus

Visited

Our House

BY T. L. OSBORN

When we were young, my wife, Daisy, and I went to India as missionaries; but we could not convince the Hindus and the Moslems that Jesus Christ is God's Son and that He was raised from the dead. They asked us to prove it. I read verses from our Bible to them; but they had their Koran, which they claimed was God's word, given by the mouth of his prophet, Mohammed.

Both books, the Bible and the Koran, were beautiful black books with gold embossed letters on their covers.

Which was God's Word?

We could not prove the Bible to be God's Word, because we did not understand faith and the need for miracles at that time. So we returned to America in what seemed to be defeat.

But we had seen the masses, and we knew they needed to believe the good news of Jesus Christ in order to be saved. We fasted and prayed many days for God to show us His answer to our dilemma. How were we to help non-Christians to believe on Jesus Christ, to be convinced that He is more than just another religion?

> *I lay before Jesus as though I were dead.*

God answered our prayer.

One morning at six o'clock, Jesus Christ awakened me in our bedroom. I lay before Him as though I were dead, unable to move a finger or toe. Water poured from my eyes, yet I was not conscious of weeping.

After a long while, I was able to crawl from my bed to the floor where I lay on my face until the afternoon.

When I walked out of that room, I was a new man. Jesus became Lord and Master of my life. I knew this truth: He is alive! He is more than a religion!

Soon after that awesome experience, a man of God came to our area. He had an amazing gift of healing. As we attended his meetings, we saw hundreds accept Christ; and right before our eyes, we watched him cast out devils and lay hands on the sick in Jesus Christ's name. The blind, deaf, dumb, and cripples were healed instantly.

A thousand voices whirled over my head, saying, *"You can do that. That is what Peter and Paul did. That is what Jesus did. That proves that the Bible is true. You can do that."*

As we walked out of that packed auditorium, we were overwhelmed.

We began fasting and praying again. Daisy and I made a new pact with God. We resolved that we would read the New Testament as though we had never read it before in our lives; and we would believe everything we read.

Whatever Jesus told us to do as His followers, we would do. Whatever He said He would do, we would expect Him to do.

We would act upon His written word, just as prophets of God acted upon His spoken word in Bible days.

We would do as the first disciples of our Lord had done.

If He said we could heal the sick, we would expect to see the sick healed.

If He said we could cast out devils, then we would do it in His name and expect them to obey us.

I can never tell you what that step meant to us. The Bible became a living, pulsating, thrilling book of truth.

We disregarded all of the teaching we had ever had. We accepted God's Word as being true and began to act on it exactly like the early Christian believers did.

Through that decision, we discovered the authority we have in the name of Jesus and the power we have over the kingdom of Satan, as well as the virtue that flows through every true believer. . . .

I can witness that, for nearly four decades, in seventy nations of the world, Daisy and I have gone in Jesus' name and have acted on the written word of God.

We have preached to multitudes—from 10,000 to over 200,000 souls daily in these mass crusades—and have seen tens of thousands of the most amazing miracles perhaps ever witnessed in any Christian ministry. . . .

. . . A man came to me asking that we pray for him to be healed. He had been deaf in one ear for over twenty years.

He seemed to be very uncertain regarding his healing, because as he put it: "I've been prayed for by the greatest people of faith in our country during the last twenty years, and I have never received help." Then he asked, "Why cannot my ear be healed?"

"It can," I replied, "if you will believe."

"But they have all told me that," he said, "and I have never received help from any of them."

"My friend," I interrupted, "do you think God is willing to heal a fellow like you?"

"I don't know," he answered; then added, "I know that if it is His will to do it, He is able, but—well, I guess that's just one of those things we aren't supposed to know."

I said, "That is why you have never been healed. You have never read the Word of God for yourself, nor have you received the faith that has been taught to you. You do not know whether or not God has said He would heal you; therefore, you do not know whether or not it is His will to heal you."

I asked, "Do you believe it is God's will to keep His promise?"

"Of course," he replied.

"Well," I said, "He has promised to heal you; and if I can quote you His promise, then you should believe Him and be healed right here and now."

I quoted a few Scriptures regarding the healing of our bodies, which are applicable to everyone individually, such as "I am the Lord who heals *you*," which was spoken to over three million people; "By whose stripes *you* were healed," and "Is *any* sick among you? Let that person call." Then I asked, "Now, in the face of all of these Scriptures, which are statements made to all who will believe them, do you think God included you?"

"Yes," he said, "I guess He did."

"Well then," I asked, "is God willing to heal you, seeing that He has made provision for the healing of every sickness and every disease among all the people?"

"Yes," he said, very firmly. "I do believe healing is for me tonight. I have never seen it like this before."

There seemed to be a glitter of faith in his eyes when he saw that God's Word was for him personally.

I knew the circumstances were right for prayer on his behalf. I had hardly touched his deaf ear before sound burst into it and he could hear me as well with that ear as with the other.

When, at last, he knew what God had said regarding all sickness and disability, and dared to step out on that word, declaring himself as being included in the *any* of James 5:14, the *you* of Exodus 15:26, and the *our* of Matthew 8:17, then what God's word had said was accomplished in him. He was healed.

> And it came to pass, as Peter passed throughout all quarters, he came down also to the saints which dwelt at Lydda. And there he found a certain man named Aeneas, which had kept his bed eight years, and was sick of the palsy. And Peter said unto him, Aeneas, Jesus Christ maketh thee whole: arise, and make thy bed. And he arose immediately.
>
> —Acts 9:32–34 KJV

217

Lord,

Praise You, O my soul; I will not forget all Your benefits—You forgive all my sins and heal all my diseases, You redeem my life from the pit and crown me with love and compassion.

Amen

$\mathcal{J}$ust in $\mathcal{T}$ime

BY MICHAEL S. BOLLEY

In 1968 I was privileged to be part of a five-person team sent to South America for three months. Our purpose was to be involved in special music ministry activities that summer. For whatever reason (maybe I looked like an accountant!) I was placed in charge of the group's funds. We traveled almost constantly—seldom staying more than a day or two in one place. As we traveled, it was my responsibility to manage the team's cash to cover our expenses.

About a week before we were scheduled to leave South America and return to the United States, I was informed that before we would be allowed to board the plane to go home we would have to pay an "airport tax." For the five of us, that would amount to about

$25 (US). In those days and in that place, $25 was a substantial sum of money.

When I heard the news, I knew we were in trouble—the treasury had only about $5 in it and we still had several days before departure—and more expenses. I had never heard of an "airport tax," and certainly had not budgeted for it. My initial thought was to start planning how to contact our sponsors back in the States and get them to wire us $25. But that would be tough to do, considering where we were and our schedule.

We needed $25 to board the plane for home and we had only about $5.

The next morning our team held its daily "staff meeting" to discuss our activities and pray together. I told the others about our situation. We decided to see what God would do. We had no means of raising that kind of money, and we did not want to burden the people we were serving with our problem. We decided to keep the situation to ourselves.

I felt strangely calmed as we prayed together, putting the problem at God's feet, saying, "It's all Yours."

The following day I was handed an envelope addressed to the team from some people with whom we had worked in another city a few weeks before. In the envelope was a nice letter dated about the same time that I had discovered our need. The letter stated that the people had closed the books on their project and had some funds left over. They wished to send these excess funds to us to help with any needs we might have. This was an extremely generous gesture!

With the letter was a check in exactly the right amount to cover our need—$25.

As a group, we composed and signed a letter of thanks to these people who had listened to God's prompting. We shared with them the story of how God had used their obedience and generosity in such a gracious way.

Coincidence? Perhaps. But it is a coincidence with God's fingerprints all over it.

> The LORD will guide you always; he will satisfy your needs in a sun-scorched land and will strengthen your frame. You will be like a well-watered garden, like a spring whose waters never fail.
>
> —Isaiah 58:11

Lord,

I give thanks to You for Your unfailing love and Your wonderful deeds, for You satisfy the thirsty and fill the hungry with good things.

Amen

*L*ord, What

*D*o *I* *T*ell

*M*y Son?

By A. Koshy Muthalaly

I t was a cold and icy Christmas morning. Our son Alex was about six or seven. He dashed downstairs to the Christmas tree in the corner of the living room.

I expected him to tear open the presents.

Instead, he stood in silence, ignoring his presents under the tree. He reached for a little saucer.

How did that get there? I wondered.

As Alex picked up the saucer, I saw disappointment all over his face.

He had left a cookie on the saucer the previous night before he went to bed! We hadn't noticed the cookie "for Santa" or the note along with it. He had even lifted the window shutter a little bit, "so that Santa could come in."

The uneaten cookie told him that Santa hadn't come to see him. On the little scrap of paper, he had scribbled in his own broken handwriting, "Dear Santa, please take away my hearing aids."

I felt helpless.

Alex had lost some of his hearing and wanted so much to be like his friends. Santa seemed to be his answer.

We hadn't seen the cookie and note Alex left for Santa.

I was at a loss for words. I prayed silently for wisdom, and then I grabbed him in my arms and propped him on my lap and tried to explain a difficult situation. But I knew I was not doing a good job. Santa had let him down, and I did not know how to help.

I tried to keep back the tears that were welling up inside me as I held him close and sought to comfort him. I felt powerless, but he held on to me as we sobbed together.

Children forget their pain so quickly; in fact, Alex doesn't even remember that Christmas disappointment.

My own pain upon seeing his disappointment stayed with me and haunted me. I have never felt so utterly vulnerable before or since.

The Bible reminds us Jesus gave up His power so that we could be empowered in our times of weakness. He made Himself nothing so that we could become something. I believe Jesus was there in my time of weakness, and He removed the disappointment from my child's memory.

In his helplessness, little Alex turned to his earthly father for comfort. In my pain I turned to my heavenly Father for consolation. My vulnerability was an open door for His hope, and in my weakness I found the strength He promises.

As I write this, Alex is twenty years old and attending college and doing well. Today, I still find myself in situations where I have to ask, *"Lord, what do I tell my son?"* I don't have all the answers, but I know that He does.

> In the same way, the Spirit helps us in our weakness. We do not know what we ought to pray for, but the Spirit himself intercedes for us with groans that words cannot express.

—Romans 8:26

Lord,

You are my strength and my impenetrable shield; my heart trusts in, relies on, and confidently leans on You, and I am helped.

Amen

$\mathcal{M}$iracle

on
$\mathcal{P}$eck Road

By Mary Marcia Lee Norwood

I was a teacher at a growing Christian school in Independence, Missouri. We held classes in Waldo Avenue Baptist Church, but we were cramped.

My husband, Ed, and I drove past the Frank X. Wachter School at 105 Peck Road many times.

On April 29, 1982, I had an overwhelming desire to stop the car and take a closer look at the school. Our two children, Kristin (ten years old) and Benjamin (six years old), were with me that day. Traffic zoomed past us as we got out of our car and stood amid the tall grass and dandelions. It was apparent that school was not being held in the building. My mind raced with possibilities.

"Let's pray!" I said.

At first Kristin and Ben were hesitant, but they agreed to join hands as I prayed out loud.

If I had formed the words in my mind *before* I prayed, I would have asked God to help us *buy* the building for our church and Christian school. But the words that came out of my mouth surprised me. I said, "Thank you, God, for giving us this building."

God planted seeds of possibility in my mind.

> *The words of my prayer surprised me. I had not intended to ask for the building.*

We prayed again and claimed the school building for Jesus. I humbly asked God to give us some "news" by the end of two weeks. I noted the name, Frank X. Wachter, on the building and 1943 as the date on the cornerstone. The next day I contacted the office of the school board in Independence, Missouri, and the school board's attorney to discover the legal status of the school.

They informed me the building could *not* be sold, as they had been unable to locate any Wachter heirs since the district closed the building in 1976.

"Great!" I said. "Because God is going to give us the building." Once again my mouth proclaimed a promise that only God could fulfill.

I shared the vision the Lord gave me with our pastor, Dr. William O. Poe of Waldo Avenue Baptist Church. He added his faith to mine. We prayed together and believed God for a miracle.

Fellow teachers at Independence Christian School and I took our students to the vacated Wachter School grounds. With hearts and hands united, we asked God to give us the vacant, four-room schoolhouse. What a sight we must have been to the people in the cars and buses that passed by. The prayers of the precious three-, four-, and five-year-old boys and girls did not go unnoticed by our heavenly Father.

The faith and prayers of other believers energized me. The promises in God's Word encouraged me to believe that God could do the impossible! I claimed Hebrews 11:1: "Faith is the substance of things hoped for, the evidence of things unseen" (KJV).

I kept notes on what God did. Here's a synopsis of the events.

May 3, 1982: I searched for any surviving Wachter heirs by writing letters to everyone named Wachter in the Kansas City telephone book.

May 11, 1982: Our daughter, Kristin, said, "Mom, do we have to clean the Wachter School tonight or wait for the weekend?" Kristin's childlike faith *already* believed that the building was ours.

May 12, 1982: I was contacted by William Wachter. He had received one of my letters. Although he was not a direct heir, he gave me the name and address of Raymond J. Wachter, a surviving Wachter heir. This was the heir the school district said they could not locate. God sent us this news on the evening of the thirteenth day. (Our original prayer requested news by the end of two weeks!)

May 13, 1982: I went to the Office of Records at the Court House in Independence, Missouri. One of the clerks said she attended Wachter School as a child. I discovered the actual Warranty Deed for the Frank X. Wachter School, dated 1943. A reversion clause in the deed stated that if the school was not used for school purposes, then ownership reverted back to the heirs of Ernestine and Frank X. Wachter!

May 14, 1982: It rained so hard it was difficult to keep the car on the road as I drove to the post office to mail a letter to Raymond J. Wachter. I advised him of the reversion clause and included a copy of the original 1943 Warranty Deed.

I wrote the following words to him: "I do not have the funds to purchase the Frank X. Wachter School. I am looking to God to supply our needs. If it is within your power to do so, please consider this request: Is there any reason why you could not *give* this building and the grounds to Independence Christian School?"

May 18, 1982: Benjamin had a dream that we were inside the Wachter School and the door was open. "It means God will give us the school," Ben said with assurance.

> *"My dream means God will give us the school,"* Ben said.

May 25, 1982: Raymond Wachter wrote a letter to me. I received the letter on Friday, June 4, 1982. He said he was unable to resolve the situation. There were many people that needed to be contacted, a few whose whereabouts were unknown. Everyone would have to agree to donate the school to us. He said he would try.

February 18, 1983: Raymond Wachter and his niece, Joan Kissick, visited Independence Christian School at Waldo Avenue Baptist Church. We held a special assembly in their honor. Children from preschool up to sixth grade participated.

February 22, 1983: Raymond Wachter wrote to thank the children for the assembly. He added, "Let us have patience. I believe, with God's help, this can be worked out to our mutual satisfaction and advantage."

At last, two years after my first prayer, Raymond Wachter and his niece, Joan Kissick, and her husband, Bob Kissick, contacted all the descendants of Ernestine J. Wachter. They *all* agreed to donate the Frank X. Wachter School to Waldo Avenue Baptist Church.

March 12, 1984: In a letter to me, Raymond Wachter wrote, "It is our prayer that God will rededicate the grounds and building for a religious education for many generations of Independence children."

May 1984: One of the thank you notes from a fourth grade student said:

Dear Wachter Family,

Thank you for donating the Wachter School to our school. We appreciate it very much. It seems like a miracle. To us, you are a blessing in disguise from God. Independence Christian School is growing larger every year. You gave the building to us right when we needed it. God bless you. You are a very good family.

In God's Love,
Tammy

Therefore I tell you, whatever you ask for in prayer, believe that you have received it, and it will be yours.

—Mark 11:24

Lord,

*You are able to do immeasurably more
than all I ask or imagine, according to
Your power that is at work within. You,
alone, shall receive the glory.*

Amen

A Word of Knowledge

By Richard Roberts, adapted by Jan Dargatz

Richard Roberts knew that he was called to be in ministry from the time he was a teenager, but for years he thought the fulfillment of that call was in a singing ministry. Then came the day he had the flu and returned home from a singing tour. His father, Oral Roberts came to pray for him.

As Oral prayed he began to prophesy, saying, "I see you in great auditoriums. I see you in great stadiums. I see you before kings and queens and ambassadors."

Richard knew that this dimension of ministry likely meant having a preaching and healing ministry as his father had, but he didn't feel either prepared or interested in such a calling at that time.

Years passed. In the late seventies, Richard appeared on a well-known Christian television program and one of the other guests on the program began to prophesy over him. The person said, "The dream God has birthed in your heart of a healing ministry is coming to pass, except you won't lay your hands on the sick nearly as much as your father has. Instead, I will manifest a gift of the Spirit, the word of knowledge, and you will speak and people will be healed. It has been the cry of your heart."

> *The other guest on the TV show began prophesying about Richard.*

Richard knew this to be true. His greatest heart's desire from the time he was a child watching his father in the healing crusades had been a desire to see people saved and healed. Richard and his wife, Lindsay, began to pray, "God, whenever it's Your time, we're ready. Whenever it's Your time . . ." Richard also began to study the Bible and pray in greater earnestness, especially reading every verse in the Scriptures that dealt with healing.

The words of Mark 11:22–24 were meaningful to him: "Have faith in God. For assuredly, I say to you, whoever says to this mountain, 'Be removed and be cast into the sea,' and does not doubt in his heart, but believes that those things he says will be done, he will have whatever he says. Therefore I say to you, whatever things you ask when you pray, believe that you receive them, and you will have them."

Richard and Lindsay agreed in prayer, "By faith, God, we receive a healing ministry." Every day, they thanked God for giving Richard a healing ministry, even though there was no evidence yet of such a ministry.

Several months later Richard was nearing the close of a service at which hundreds had given their lives to Jesus. He asked the people to stand for the prayer of benediction, and as He prayed, he suddenly felt prompted to say, "And Lord, heal that man's big toe."

He shook his head immediately afterward, wondering, *Why in the world did I say that?* He recognized, however, that he had spoken words God had given to him. He closed the service and went home.

A few days later, Richard received a letter from a man who had been at the service. He asked, "How did you know about my toe? I had been to the doctor that day and had discovered it was broken. When you prayed, my toe snapped. I went back to the doctor the next day and he took another x-ray. The first x-ray showed a break. The second one showed a perfectly normal toe with no break. What did you do?"

Richard wrote back, "I didn't do anything. God did."

That night as Richard slept, he dreamed of a man's big toe. For three nights straight he had the same dream—a big toe. After the third night of this strange dream, Richard shared the dream with Lindsay. She looked at him and said, "That's the beginning of your healing ministry! Don't despise a small beginning."

Richard said, "Yes, Lord, I receive this. This man's big toe is the beginning of my worldwide healing ministry!"

Through the years since that day, tens of thousands of people have written to Richard and Lindsay Roberts, telling how God healed them in live meetings and on television after they heard a spoken "word of knowledge" and received a prayer of faith.

The prophetic words spoken over Richard's life have come to fulfillment. In more than a half dozen nations where he has held crusades, Richard has conducted his meetings directly at the invitation of the president or monarch of the nation. He has spoken in great auditoriums and stadiums to audiences that have numbered in the hundreds of thousands.

God speaks through people to plant his dreams in human hearts. He speaks through people to cause faith to rise for healing. Yes, He speaks through people to accomplish His purposes on this earth!

> For you know that we dealt with each of you as a father deals with his own children, encouraging, comforting and urging you to live lives worthy of God, who calls you into his kingdom and glory. And we also thank God continually because, when you received the word of God, which you heard from us, you accepted it not as the word of men, but as it actually is, the word of God, which is at work in you who believe.
>
> —1 Thessalonians 2:11–13

Lord,

**You are the God of peace.
You equip me with everything good for
doing Your will. Please work in me what is
pleasing to You, through Jesus Christ.**

Amen

$\mathscr{L}$earning

to Hear
$\mathscr{H}$isVoice

By Michael R. Wells

As a young Christian I was blessed to grow up around believers who were constantly coming up with words from God. Since 1 Corinthians 14:1 says we are to "eagerly desire spiritual gifts, especially the gift of prophecy," I set out to learn to hear from God and speak His words.

It wasn't long after I had made my commitment that I had an opportunity to speak God's words at my job. Early one morning a fellow employee named Dan showed up to work with a slightly swollen eye. I believed that I was to pray for Dan, but I avoided asking if I could do so. Finally, I said, *"Lord, if I am to pray for Dan then You need to tell me what to say."*

I sensed the Lord say to me, *"Pray, 'Let it fall out.'"*

Give me a break! I thought. *Let* what *fall out?*

I decided this was not the voice of the Lord. But the prompting would not go away. No amount of arguing about how stupid it would be to pray such a ridiculous prayer would quiet that still, small voice.

Finally, I gave in and went upstairs to find Dan.

When I told my nonbelieving friend that I wanted to pray for his eye, he was surprisingly open. I explained that God had given some rather specific instructions and that was how I was going to pray. My prayer went something like this, "Father, I thank You that You care so much for Dan that You sent me to pray so his eye would be healed. Lord, I ask You to touch his eye and heal it. In Jesus' name I say, 'Let it fall out. Lord, let it fall out.'"

> *Give me a break! Let what fall out? That's so stupid. It can't be the voice of God.*

Nothing happened immediately and, to say the least, I was disappointed and a bit embarrassed. But my friend thanked me for caring enough to pray. Frankly, I thought that would be the end of the matter.

But the next morning Dan came in all excited. "You wouldn't believe what happened to me last night!" he said. "I decided to go get a beer. After I took my first drink I put it back on the bar and looked down into my glass. Suddenly a grain of sand popped out of my bad eye and fell right into my beer. And look, my eye is all better now."

Dan was deeply touched by the whole incident and even spoke of turning his life over to the Lord and quitting drinking. And what a great faith builder for me! Because I was faithful in a little "foolishness," God was able to touch a man's life in ways I could never have imagined.

> How shall we escape if we ignore such a great salvation? This salvation, which was first announced by the Lord, was confirmed to us by those who heard him. God also testified to it by signs, wonders and various miracles, and gifts of the Holy Spirit distributed according to his will.

—Hebrews 2:3–4

Lord,

I will remember Your deeds; yes, I will remember Your miracles of long ago. I will meditate on all Your works and consider all Your mighty deeds. You are the God Who performs miracles.

Amen

God's Dark Room

By Lynn D. Morrissey

January was a bleak month. My husband, Michael, had suffered a heart attack and nearly died, and I learned that my beloved great-aunt, Martha, was dying. My hope, like the amaryllis bulb I'd just planted in a pot on the kitchen windowsill, lay buried beneath ugly fears. I entered God's "dark room."

I anguished over Martha's rapidly deteriorating health. Colon cancer ravished her body with unrelenting fury, causing her once-supple skin to shrivel tightly over her angular skeleton. Yet, somehow the greater her pain and weakness became, the greater her determination to live. Martha had an indomitable spirit, a generous heart, and an inexhaustible capacity for joy—but she wasn't a Christian.

The closer she came to death, the more I feared for her salvation. Whenever I talked about God, she grew uncomfortable. Now, with no time to lose, I prayed whenever I was with Martha. Each time, she pushed me away, saying, "Please stop, honey. You're scaring me."

Out of respect for her, I did stop but sensed God's disapproval.

"Pray anyway," God said. "She will die without Jesus."

In the hospital Michael and I met a wonderful chaplain named Jim who agreed to visit Martha regularly to comfort her and share the gospel. Martha looked forward to his visits and "flirted" with him in her impish, mischievous way even though she was eighty-two!

Yet, whenever Jim talked about Christ, Martha grew uneasy. She was especially frightened when he prayed.

One day before I left the nursing home, I told Martha I was going to pray for her.

Once more she pushed me away, expressing her fear.

This time I remained by her bed, strongly sensing God directing me to ask her why she was afraid.

"How can I do that, Lord? She will push me away, and that hurts—though I know she isn't upset with me. Yet, I am offending her and making her miserable."

I sensed God answer, *"How can you not? She will die without Jesus!"*

I obeyed the Lord and asked her why she was afraid.

After a long pause, her anguish spilled out: "I'm afraid of dying!"

I realized that she had equated my prayers with my knowledge of her impending death. I was so relieved to tell her that she didn't need to fear the only One Who could help her. With God's help I told her about God's way of salvation.

A couple days later Jim visited Martha. As soon as she saw him, though she was incredibly weak, she said, "Oh, no. It's you!"

Jim guessed she was half joking, but that she anticipated his talking about God. As he leaned down by her bed, Martha raised up and hugged his neck with such force that he dropped to his knees.

"I'm so afraid to die," Martha whispered in his ear.

Jim assured Martha that there was nothing to fear—that if she knew Christ when she died, she would instantly be in heaven with Him. "Do you want Jesus to save you?"

"Yes," she whispered.

Jim prayed a short prayer as Martha repeated his words.

The next day when I saw Martha, she tried to hug me but her arms collapsed by her side. She whispered, "I love you."

I sat on her bed for over an hour, stroking her hair and moistening her lips. Before I left, I asked, "May I pray with you?"

She nodded.

I held her and prayed, and this time she didn't push me away. She was completely peaceful. She smiled sweetly and radiated incredible joy. I knew that the Holy Spirit now resided in her heart. I knew that she was ready to die—ready to *live*!

When I got home I noticed emerald amaryllis shoots towering over the pot. It had been less than two months since I'd planted the bulb, and I was amazed by the leaves' skyrocketing growth. I was anxious to see the red blooms promised by the potting instructions.

The next day we got a call from my cousin to say that Martha had died the night before, shortly after Michael and I had left her. I felt nothing. I couldn't cry.

The morning of the funeral as I filled the tea kettle at the kitchen sink, I looked up to see three bright crimson blossoms.

The amaryllis "trumpets" had bloomed simultaneously, joyously heralding the home-going of my aunt. To me, they represented the Father, Son, and Holy Spirit, keeping their promise to welcome Martha in love. Suddenly, my tears flowed.

In the days following Martha's death, I thought often about God's "dark room." Why would the Father of Lights sequester His children in darkness?

It is in the "dark night of our souls" that God's glory has the opportunity to shine brightest. It is here that He does His best work, causing even the worst of trials to work together for our good, while developing the image of His Son onto ours.

I considered how light and life paradoxically spring from darkness and death—how silver linings peek beneath dark clouds, butterflies flutter from cocoons, photographic images surface in dark rooms, and amaryllises emerge from clod-covered bulbs.

I realized that although Aunt Martha had endured one of the longest, most excruciating deaths possible, God had used her suffering to cause her to reach out to Him for salvation when she might not have otherwise. Her suffering was a "momentary, light affliction" compared with the eternal joy she was now experiencing in heaven. And I have experienced the joy of knowing that God used my small obedience in His eternal design.

> Turn, O Lord, and deliver me; save me because of your unfailing love. No one remembers you when he is dead. Who praises you from the grave? I am worn out from groaning; all night long I flood my bed with weeping and drench my couch with tears. My eyes grow weak with sorrow; they fail because of all my

foes. Away from me, all you who do evil, for the LORD has heard my weeping. The LORD has heard my cry for mercy; the LORD accepts my prayer.

—Psalm 6:4–9

Lord,

Rescue me and deliver me in Your righteousness; turn Your ear to me and save me. Be my rock of refuge, to which I can always go; give the command to save me, for You are my rock and my fortress.

Amen

$\mathcal{G}$od Knew

the

$\mathcal{W}$ay

BY MIKE EVANS, AS TOLD TO JOANN WEBSTER

As he prayed for leaders and the heads of nations, evangelist Mike Evans felt a burden for the nation of Somalia. He started praying for the unrest, the famine, and for the stationing of U.S. military personnel who were imperiled. Suddenly, he felt the Holy Spirit nudge him to go to Somalia.

Mike knew no one in that country from which to secure an invitation, so getting a visa was out of the question. He checked a map and discovered the closest airport he could legally fly into was Nairobi, Kenya, so he booked a flight and went.

Arriving on African soil, Mike hailed a taxi and started making his way to a hotel, praying aloud in the backseat. "God, I don't know how to get there, so please open a door and get me into Somalia."

"Praise the Lord, brother!" the taxi driver said.

"Do you know me?" Mike asked, bewildered.

"No, but I am a brother in Christ," the driver explained. "You want to go to Somalia? I can take you to the plane."

The taxi driver took him to a plane and Mike hopped on, assuming the cargo was food.

Mike hastily bought food to take to the starving people and then headed toward the airstrip where he saw several U.S. journalists waiting for planes that were filled with bags of what he assumed to be food. He loaded his food onto one of the planes and boarded. After takeoff and a short flight, they landed in a private airstrip in Somalia with no customs agents or police in sight.

When Mike arrived, people were rioting in the streets and the U.S. military was trying to regain order. Mike asked a group of taxi drivers waiting nearby if anyone spoke English. One did, so Mike engaged him to take him to the worst famine areas.

"You got food?" the driver asked.

"Yeah, but I guess it won't matter since the plane was filled with food."

"Food?" the driver said. "Those were drug planes!"

People flocked to Mike. Close to two hundred people were saved as Mike preached the gospel and distributed food. When he felt the burden lift, he knew it was time to return home.

At the Mogadishu airport, Mike was surrounded by armed gang members as he talked to a glassy-eyed man. Soon a crowd gathered. "Lord, I have no ticket, no way out," he breathed. "But I've trusted You, so please spare my life."

An airplane on the landing strip had just unloaded some passengers, so Mike ran to it. "How can I get a flight to Kenya?" he asked the Indian pilot.

"I'm going there now. Come with me if you want. I have no passengers."

As the plane took off, Mike watched the Somalian crowd shrink beneath him. He thought of those left behind who were praying for their nation. And he was happy the Holy Spirit had led him to be an answer to someone's prayers.

> But you are a shield around me, O LORD; you bestow glory on me and lift up my head. To the LORD I cry aloud, and he answers me from his holy hill.
>
> —Psalm 3:3–4

Lord,

You are my light and my salvation—whom shall I fear? You, Lord, are the stronghold of my life—of whom shall I be afraid?

Amen

The Spiritual Librarian

By Paige M. Kolb

I had gone into a general bookstore near my home to steal away some quiet time. It was lunch hour, so none of the big fluffy chairs were available. I ordered some coffee and parked myself at a counter seat overlooking the traffic outside. Being easily distracted in the busy café, I asked God to show me a comfy, quiet place that I could sit to prepare for the youth retreat I was leading that weekend.

I got up, walked around the bookstore, and came upon an area I hadn't noticed before. And there it was— an overstuffed chair calling my name! As I settled in and propped my feet up on the coffee table, I noticed that the Bibles and Christian book section surrounded me. I thanked God for encircling me with His Word, literally!

A few hours later, I noticed a man browsing the Bibles. I felt the Holy Spirit urging me to go over and see if he needed any help.

I can't, I thought. *I have work to do.*

The gnawing feeling didn't go away and neither did the man. By this time he was carrying three Bibles underneath his arm.

I prayed for God to lead me because I didn't know what to say or do. All I knew is that He wanted me to go over there and play like a librarian. Butterflies swirled in my stomach.

There was an overstuffed chair calling my name.

I got up and ambled toward him. "Can I help you find something?" I asked.

He looked at me strangely, especially when I told him I didn't work at the bookstore. After some nervous laughter from us both, he smiled and said he was looking for a Bible to read and wanted to make sure it had a concordance in it.

It didn't take me long to realize that he had no idea *what* a concordance was or what he was looking for. We began talking about the differences between the King James Version, New International Version, and various other versions of the Bible. I also explained what a concordance was.

In the meantime I learned that he had become a Christian the day before. My heart soared as I realized God wanted me to help this man find a Bible so that He could use it to nourish His new child. I also understood why God saved a chair for me near the Bibles; He wanted me to be His hands and feet—not just to be comfortable as I worked.

Getting out of my overstuffed "comfort zone," was worth the risk. The man finally settled on a men's devotional Bible and a leather-bound study Bible with a concordance. He thanked me for the help and was off to the checkout counter.

As I sat back down I was elated that I had obeyed the Holy Spirit's prompting to play spiritual librarian for my new brother in Christ. He was "checking out" the most important book he could ever lay his hands on!

Plans fail for lack of counsel, but with many advisers they succeed. A man finds joy in giving an apt reply— and how good is a timely word!

—Proverbs 15:22–23

Lord,

Your word that goes out from Your mouth will not return to You empty, but will accomplish what You desire and achieve the purpose for which You sent it.

Amen

More

Than

Enough

BY TROY SLEDGE

In July 1985 a team from Grace Fellowship Church went to Kenya, East Africa. I was a member on that team. The purpose of the mission trip was to provide medical and humanitarian aid to the nationals in rural Kenya, and to share the gospel.

Karen Bean, the Missions Outreach Director, led the team. Karen shared the following miracle with our team.

The northern portion of Kenya where we worked had been hit with famines. We didn't want to take food from the nationals, so I had asked the Lord's guidance for our meals. We received a donation of a large supply of powdered milk and a new food product, which wasn't available in stores—individual, vacuum-packed entrees that didn't need refrigeration. They were easy to heat in water, in the sun, or on the motor of a vehicle.

These meals would be our lunches when we held clinics. To figure how many to take we multiplied the number of team members by seven and then loaded the box to the top. We thought that was enough to cover the helpers and interpreters also. What we didn't figure was that the workers would each consume at least two or more packs a day.

We have no food for lunch next week.

Two of our women took charge of the food preparation. On Saturday the women reported to me that we would not have any meals for lunch the next week. They said the box was almost empty.

"The Lord multiplied the loaves and fishes and this is just as important," I said. "We are His disciples so He will take care of feeding us."

Monday morning I forgot to instruct the team to bring any snacks they had.

As we were setting up the clinic, the "cooks" hurried over to me. "Where did you get the new box of food?" they asked. "There is just enough food for today!

"God provided," I said, as surprised as they were.

Every day thereafter there was a fresh supply. On the last day the box was more full than normal. At the end of clinic we were able to send each worker home with a supply for their family, plus a package of powdered milk. Finally, the box was empty.

But the food miracle was not the only miracle we witnessed. One of the team members, Sabra Smith, had spent weeks making dolls to give away at our clinics. Women in the church had donated their time to help her make these small cloth dolls with embroidered hair and faces. Sabra worried that there wouldn't be enough dolls, so she had team members finishing dolls on the flight to Kenya. We packed approximately 380 dolls to distribute to small children in the African villages.

Each day there were more dolls in the bag than the day before.

We were in Kenya for almost three weeks and worked in several different villages. Sabra was responsible for giving out the dolls.

One day she came to me and said, "Something has happened that I cannot explain. Each day when I reach in the bag, there are more dolls than were there at the end of the day before."

The Lord was multiplying the dolls!

Before handing out the dolls, the team had prayed and asked God to bless all who received the dolls.

At first Sabra gave dolls only to children. But at one hospital a sick young man pulled himself to the bottom of his bed and held out his hand with eager anticipation to receive one of these blessed toys.

Why would a grown man want one of these? Sabra wondered. But she couldn't resist handing him a doll. When she did, her heart was filled with compassion as she watched the gratitude sweep his face. *It must be the blessing that he senses,* she thought, not yet realizing the miracle that was taking place.

By the end of the mission trip, we had calculated that over 800 dolls had been given to the African children—double what we had brought!

If you then, though you are evil, know how to give good gifts to your children, how much more will your Father in heaven give the Holy Spirit to those who ask him!

—Luke 11:13

Lord,

I love You with all of my heart and with all my soul and with all my strength. May Your commandments remain in my heart.

Amen

A Gift
of
Obedience

By Ben Groenewold,
as told to Jan Dargatz

I was looking forward to attending a men's retreat being sponsored by a church at a campground near the Arkansas and Oklahoma border. As the retreat date grew closer, however, I discovered I had a conflicting commitment and would be unable to attend.

During the church service on the Sunday before the retreat, I heard the Lord speak as clearly as a bell, *"Ben, give your retreat tuition."* The message was simple and direct. It was as if all other sounds became mute and everything seemed to stand still in time as I heard the voice in my spirit.

After the service was over I went to the table where Mark, the registrar for the retreat, was sitting. I wrote a check for the amount of the retreat, handed the check to Mark, and said, "Here is the money, but I'm not going to be able to go."

"Why are you giving me this check, then?" Mark asked.

"Use it as a scholarship for someone," I said, satisfied that I had fulfilled God's directive.

As my wife, Marty, and I walked away from the table, we encountered our young friend Brittain. Marty had been mentoring a group of four young women in the church, including Brittain. All of the young women were speech pathology majors, all were looking for mates, and all were eager to know and to pursue God's calling on their lives. The group had become very special to Marty, and I, too, had begun to take an interest in the futures of these young women.

"Ben, give your tuition money."

I asked if Brittain's boyfriend, Doug, was going on the men's retreat. Doug was a graduate student in a degree program preparing him for ministry.

"No," Brittain replied. "He'd really like to go but he doesn't have the money."

"Go and see Mark," I said. "I just gave him money for a scholarship."

Brittain went immediately to where Mark was sitting. He awarded the scholarship to Doug, and Doug went on what turned out to be a life-changing retreat.

At the time of his gift, I did not know that Doug was grappling with a major decision in his life. Discouraged with his studies, Doug wanted to drop his degree program and leave school. During the retreat, however, he had several talks with the retreat leaders that renewed the fire in his soul for ministry. Upon returning from the retreat, he re-enrolled in his degree program and completed the program.

Several weeks before he graduated, he and Brittain became engaged, both of them filled with enthusiasm about God's plans for their life together in ministry.

I was overjoyed when I heard how God had used my gift to renew the call of God on a young man's life. There was no doubt about what God wanted done, I didn't even stop to ask why. I knew there was only one response to such a clear directive from God and that was obedience.

> Because of the service by which you have proved yourselves, men will praise God for the obedience that accompanies your confession of the gospel of Christ, and for your generosity in sharing with them and with everyone else.
>
> —2 Corinthians 9:13

Lord,

You, O God, are strong and loving. Surely You will reward each person according to what he has done.

Amen

From Boredom
to
*B*oldness

BY DR. LLOYD OGILVIE

The Library of Congress once sponsored a magnificent exhibit of pictures and artifacts on the development of religion in America. The display began with paintings of scenes of religious persecution in England, Scotland, and on the continent, which prompted the early immigration to America.

I was startled when I saw the first illustration: a drawing of the 1615 Glasgow martyring of John Ogilvie, the only post-Reformation Roman Catholic to be martyred in Scotland. He died a gruesome death. I remembered that John Ogilvie had left the Calvinist persuasion to become a Jesuit priest. There are conflicting stories about the nature of the crime for which he was martyred. Some say he was caught saying the Mass; others indicate that he was punished for treasonous plotting against James VI.

The memory of John Ogilvie is not dead, however. Some years ago, a man by the name of John Fagan was healed of cancer by wearing a medallion of Blessed John Ogilvie. Fagan's wife prayed for Ogilvie's healing, and her husband was cured. This made Blessed John a candidate for sainthood by the Vatican. After a thorough investigation of his life, miracles, and sacrificial service, he was indeed elevated to sainthood.

What began as a joke became serious cause for reflection.

About that time, while I was still a pastor in Hollywood, California, a friend of mine sent me a book entitled *Blessed John Ogilvie, Martyred in Scotland* and an article about the canonization. Another friend changed the title of the book cover to read *Lloyd John Ogilvie, Martyred in Hollywood*. We both laughed about that. But then we had a serious conversation about what *we* would be willing to die for. Saint John Ogilvie had stirred up some challenging reflections.

In America we enjoy spiritual freedom. But what if we lost that blessing and it became a crime to be a Christian? If we were brought to trial, what evidence, material and circumstantial, would the prosecutor be able to use to convict us? Most of us would never be brought to trial, much less convicted, because so little about what we do and say could be identified as Christ's power in us. Why is it that we find it so difficult to talk about what we believe and act on the convictions we hold dearly but never express daringly?

The word *witness* actually means "martyr." There can be no Holy Spirit empowering unless we are engaged in being witnesses in the full implication of the word's original meaning. That implies that nothing can dissuade us from our belief and confidence in Christ. It also suggests a Cross-oriented love for the people with whom we want to share the good news of Christ's love. . . . How many people in our lives know without any shadow of doubt our forgiving, accepting, and affirming love? . . .

A woman wrote me to say that she had been in a dry spell spiritually. She was anxiously seeking the power of the Holy Spirit, yet she felt no flow of new life or enthusiasm.

I asked her to tell me the names of ten people who needed love.

Each one she listed needed wisdom, knowledge, and faith, which she could not engender in them. But when she became involved in some specific, costly ways of caring for these people, *then* the Holy Spirit empowered her. She realized that she was saying things to these people beyond her human intelligence and communicating hope beyond her experience. When she became stretched by the actual demands of loving, she received a profound experience of the Holy Spirit's gift of love. She knew it; so did the people she cared for.

Her "martyrdom" did not cost her her life, but it did cost time, energy, and privacy. Her reward was an intensive, intimate experience of the Spirit of God. The same can be true for us.

> "He [Jesus] was not seen by all the people, but by witnesses whom God had already chosen—by us who ate and drank with him after he rose from the dead. He commanded us to preach to the people and to testify that he is the one whom God appointed as judge of the

living and the dead. All the prophets testify about him that everyone who believes in him receives forgiveness of sins through his name."

While Peter was still speaking these words, the Holy Spirit came on all who heard the message.

—Acts 10:41–43

Lord,

I eagerly expect and hope that I will in no way be ashamed, but will have sufficient courage so that Christ will be exalted in my body, whether by life or by death. For to me, to live is Christ and to die is gain.

Amen

GOODNESS AND MERCY FOLLOWS US

Surely or only goodness, mercy, and unfailing love shall follow me all the days of my life, and through the length of my days the house of the Lord [and His presence] shall be my dwelling place.

—Psalm 23:6 AMP

Good things happen to those who dwell in the presence of the Lord. The promise of mercy and unfailing love is a tangible picture of abundance that the Lord means for us all to enjoy. Jessica Nichols enjoyed the presence of God on the beach. Bishop Cox enjoyed a fruitful ministry as he sought the presence of God in Indonesia.

When tragedy caused tension between Dean Crowe and her dearest friends, the presence of God brought mercy and reunited the two families again. Carol Genengels tells the story of Kelly, the single mother who learned that God is so good He even cares about her laundry. Marita Littauer's story from her new book, *Love Extravagantly*, shows God cares about home decorating when we invite His presence to be made manifest in our homes. And who would have thought that an ugly cat could demonstrate the goodness of God? But Ava Chambers tells of a time when God clearly spoke to a child about her favorite pet.

Jim Wilson learned that God fills our voice with a proclamation of Good News, even when our voice has been taken away. Dana Pope's story foreshadows a day when all believers will rise up with one voice to proclaim that goodness and mercy is surely found in the house of the Lord. The closing words, from Bishop T. D. Jakes's study of Ephesians titled, *Intimacy with God*, reminds us that God works according to His power, and God is able!

God Is Not Your Problem

BY JOHN MASON

Some time ago I was eating at a Mexican fast-food restaurant. As I stood in line for service I noticed in front of me a very poor elderly lady who looked like a street person. When it came her turn, she ordered some water and one taco. As I sat in the booth right next to her, I couldn't help but observe and be moved with compassion toward her. Shortly after I had begun my meal I went over to her and asked if I could buy some more food for her lunch. She looked at me and angrily asked, "Who are you?"

"Just a guy who wants to help you," I responded.

She ignored me.

I finished my meal about the same time she did, and we both got up to leave. I felt led to give her some money. In the parking lot I approached her and offered her some cash.

Her only response to me was, "Stop bothering me." Then, she stormed off.

Immediately, the Lord showed me that this is often the way many of us respond to Him. When He calls out to us, seeking to bless us, we act as though we don't even know Who He is. We respond to His offer of blessing by asking, "Who are You? What do You want from me?" The Lord, being the gracious God He is, continues to try to bless us. Yet we react by saying, "Stop bothering me." We walk off, just as this lady did, missing out on the rich blessings of the Lord.

It's not the absence of problems that gives us peace; it's God's presence with us in the problems. . . . In Romans 8:38–39 the apostle Paul writes, "For I am convinced that neither death nor life, neither angels nor demons, neither present nor the future, nor any powers, neither height nor depth, nor anything else in all creation, will be able to separate us from the love of God that is in Christ Jesus our Lord." In verse 31 Paul declares, "What, then, shall we say in response to this? If God is for us, who can be against us?" A paraphrase might be, "If God is for us, who cares who is against us?"

In Psalm 145:18 we read, "The Lord is near to all who call on him, to all who call on him in truth." James 4:8 admonishes us, "Come near to God and he will come near to you."

Thank God that we can, without hesitation and with full confidence, lean on His eternal faithfulness.

Before they call I will answer; while they are still speaking I will hear.

—Isaiah 65:24

Lord,

I give thanks to You for I will not work in
vain, and my heirs are not doomed to
misfortune, for we are a people blessed
by You.

Amen

God's
Heartbeat

By Jessica Nichols

W henever I get an opportunity to go to the beach, I listen for it—the heartbeat of God. For some reason, I expect to hear it there better than anywhere else on earth. The longing to hear the heartbeat of God is the cry of my heart.

Because I live in the desert, visits to the beach are rare. But the year of our twenty-fifth anniversary, my husband, Mike, gave me something special, something that he would not normally give. (The beach is *my* favorite place, not his.) He took me to South Padre Island in southern Texas.

My heart did flip-flops the whole way there; I was excited to smell the salt air, feel the warm sun on my skin, and squish the sand between my toes all the way up to my knees if I could. I wanted to talk to God on the beach, to hear Him speak to me, to see Him in a whole new way. It took fourteen hours to get there.

Once there, the salty air was more fragrant than I had remembered, the sun on my skin made every cell in my being stand and thank God for its beauty and warmth. This day was special. It was my twenty-fifth wedding anniversary, twelve days before my forty-fifth birthday, and I was at my favorite spot on earth with the love of my life.

> *I always know and understand God better at the beach.*

Standing on the warm sand, I asked God the question I had been waiting to ask: *"OK, what does 'it' sound like? You know, Your heartbeat? That rhythmic noise that every human has inside, that one thing that none of us can live without—what does Your heartbeat sound like?"*

I stood there waiting, listening, but all I could hear was the pounding of the waves.

I looked around me at thousands of people who appeared to be oblivious to God.

Then it happened—a rush of compassion for those thousands of people. All of a sudden I wondered, *"Do they know You? Have they heard of You, Jesus?"* I wanted to jump up and scream to all of them, "Do you know that Jesus died for you and that your sins are in a big sea, just like this one, forgiven and forgotten?"

Then that still, small voice started speaking—the gentle stirring within that is undeniably God. *"That's it, Jessica. That's My heartbeat. I have no grandchildren, no nieces, nephews, only sons and daughters. My heartbeat sounds like—more children, more children, more children. If you want to hear My heartbeat, bring Me more children."*

I cried and asked forgiveness for not being a grateful child and bringing Him more children. He wants more children, not because He is selfish, but because He *loves* them. It is God's will that *none* should perish.

I cried too because I had heard what I wanted to hear—His heartbeat.

> The Lord is not slow in keeping his promise, as some understand slowness. He is patient with you, not wanting anyone to perish, but everyone to come to repentance.
>
> —2 Peter 3:9

Lord,

Surely You will gather us all, You will collect us, Your children, and bring us together like sheep in a fold. Let my heart beat as Yours with love for my brothers and sisters.

Amen

$\mathcal{P}$raying for $\mathcal{G}$uidance

BY BISHOP WILLIAM COX,
AS TOLD TO JAN DARGATZ

Several years ago Bishop William Cox and other clergy and laypersons gathered at Claggett Conference Center in Maryland for an all-day seminar and practicum on evangelism. The featured speaker was Edwin Stube, an Episcopal priest who had been a missionary in Indonesia. He shared with the group his method of evangelism, which he believed to be in keeping with the method used by Jesus' disciples, as well as those in the early church.

While in Indonesia, Father Stube had visited a number of villages for the purpose of evangelism. He and

269

others with him would stand in the main road leading into the village and pray, "Where are we supposed to go, Lord, to minister today?"

As they prayed, the Lord would always draw their attention to a particular house. Invariably, they would go to the home and be invited in. They nearly always found someone who was ill or in need and they would pray for the person in the name of Jesus. They had many miraculous encounters.

Meanwhile, the children who lived at the home where the encounters occurred would run through the village and tell the news of what was happening at their house. The entire village would gather together and Father Stube and his team would have the opportunity to preach. People came to Christ in every village they visited!

The group at the conference center was challenged to put this method to the test. They prayed, asking the Lord to show them specifically where they might go that day as teams of two to talk to people about Jesus. For every two people who went out, two others agreed to stay behind at the conference center to intercede for them.

Bishop Cox sat in prayer for more than an hour waiting on the Lord to show him where he should go. Finally, he saw a house in his mind's eye. It was a two-story house with a white picket fence in front. He clearly saw steps going up to the porch, which sat back from the fence about thirty feet. He had never seen the house before.

Then, as he continued in prayer, he saw a street. The Bishop recognized it as a side street in a community that he had visited. The street went to the left and up a hill. While he had seen the street before, he had never explored it. He knew in his spirit, however, that the house he had been shown would be on that street.

Bishop Cox and his partner drove to this community about ten miles away, and, sure enough, as they drove up the street they saw the house on the left side of the street. The house appeared just as Bishop Cox envisioned it.

They went to the door and knocked.

A man came to the door.

Bishop Cox explained that they had been praying about to whom they should go to tell the good news about Jesus Christ, and that their prayers had led them to his home.

"That's fine," the man responded. "But I have an appointment, and I am already late. I'd be happy to talk to you if you come again. But I think you are supposed to go to the house across the street. The family there has a child who was critically injured in an automobile accident this week. None of them go to church."

Bishop Cox and his partner thanked the man and walked across the street.

The family there welcomed them in and told them about recent events in their lives.

Bishop Cox and his partner prayed for the parents and for the child's recovery, and then they told the family that they felt sure they would be welcomed warmly at the Episcopal church in the community.

The family members began to attend the church, and in the end, not only did their child recover, but all five members of the family accepted Christ, were baptized, and became a part of that church body.

The Lord does not always speak in words but sometimes in visual messages to direct His people to the places He has chosen for their witness. "Where do you want us to go to minister to people in Your name?" is always a good question to ask the Lord in prayer!

For the Son of Man came to seek and to save what was lost.

—Luke 19:10

Lord,

You guide me in the way of wisdom and lead me along straight paths. When I walk, my steps will not be hampered; when I run, I will not stumble. I will hold on to Your instruction.

Amen

The Fall

BY DEAN CROWE

I wasn't prepared for what I encountered when I walked into the recovery room. There lay eight-year-old Thomas—all fifty-five pounds of him. His head was clean shaven and bandaged, and tubes were sticking into and out of his body.

I burst into tears and said, "I am so sorry! I cannot believe this happened to him while he was in my care."

Thomas and my son, Jonathan, had been best friends since they were born. We had known his parents, Cheryl and Banks, for years. They were some of our closest and dearest friends when we lived in Columbus.

About a year after we moved back to Atlanta, Thomas and his younger brother, Wilson, came to visit us for a few days. Having four boys under nine years of age was a lively affair. I was a full-time cook, chauffeur, referee, and master of ceremonies for this gang. It was great fun seeing the boys together again—just like old times.

One afternoon I needed to run some errands. I didn't expect to be gone long, so I called Bill, a teenage boy from next door, to watch the boys. He agreed and asked permission to take them to his home to show them his pet ferrets.

> *I didn't expect to be gone long, and I thought the boys would enjoy seeing Bill's ferrets.*

When I got home the boys weren't outside or in the house, so I phoned Bill's house. Bill said Thomas had fallen and they would be right over.

When they got home, Bill explained that Thomas had leaned against the side wall at the top of the stairs, misjudged the height of the wall, flipped over the wall and fallen to the floor below. Bill assured me, as did all the boys, Thomas included, that no one was roughhousing or even near Thomas when he fell. It was a complete accident.

Thomas looked tired and hungry, and he had quite a bump on his head. I gave him the how-many-fingers-am-I-holding-up vision test and he seemed quite alert. I called his mom and she said to make sure his pupils were dilating. They were. I was also relieved to see him eat two ham sandwiches and drink a glass of milk. Afterwards, he went upstairs to take a nap.

While Thomas was sleeping, I went over to Bill's house to see just how far Thomas had fallen. When I stood at the top of the stairs and listened to Bill describe what had happened, I was horrified. Thomas had fallen about nine feet onto a concrete floor.

When I got home my husband, Reid, had just arrived from work. I quickly explained the situation to him and suggested we take Thomas to the emergency room. I called Thomas's father, Banks, a physician, and told him Thomas had fallen onto a concrete floor! He asked lots of questions about Thomas's condition and decided that a trip to the emergency room would be premature.

As the afternoon progressed to evening, Thomas continued to sleep soundly. I'd wake him periodically and check his vision and ask him questions—he was always alert. Banks had assured me on the phone that everything would "probably" be OK; yet, I still had a hard time leaving Thomas's side. All I could do was hold his hand and pray over him.

Sometime after dinner, Cheryl called to say that she and Banks had decided to drive up to Atlanta to get Thomas. My heart began to race. I knew that Banks was very protective when it came to his sons.

About nine o'clock, Thomas woke up complaining of a terrible headache.

Soon Banks and Cheryl arrived.

The moment Banks saw his son, I felt his anger toward me.

He grabbed Thomas and his belongings, and in a flash they were in the car and ready to go.

Just before getting into the car, Cheryl took my hands, looked me straight in the eyes, and said, "God knew before Thomas was even born that this was going to happen. He is in control. The Lord knows the number of hairs on Thomas's head. He is God's child.

"And Banks—he'll be OK. He just needs some time." She kissed me and got in the car.

Despite her words of comfort and trust, I was certain that Banks held me solely responsible for Thomas's injury. I wanted to die. *"Why did this have to happen, Lord?"* I prayed. *"Why?"*

After a restless night, I called Cheryl about 6 A.M. My heart sank when a baby-sitter answered the phone.

She informed me that Thomas had started vomiting at about 5:00 that morning and they had taken him to the emergency room.

Banks called shortly after with news from the hospital. Thomas had suffered a cracked skull, had an epidermal hematoma, and would be going into surgery soon.

I was numb. I felt totally responsible for Thomas's accident. *"Is this the end of our friendship, Lord?"* I cried. *"Why must it end this way!"*

> *Must our friendship end? Why did this happen, Lord?*

I was crying so hard that I could barely speak; yet, somehow I managed to call my mom and some dear friends to pray. They called other prayer warriors and soon folks all over Atlanta, Columbus, and Birmingham were praying for Thomas.

As Reid and I headed for Columbus, I dreaded seeing Banks.

When we arrived we found Cheryl in the surgical recovery unit and she assured us that the surgery had gone well.

"Thomas will be fine," she said.

I thanked the Lord.

Reid went upstairs to the pediatric intensive care unit where Banks was preparing Thomas's room.

Cheryl took me into Thomas's recovery room. Through tears, I gazed at Thomas with his shaven head and tubes everywhere. I stroked his feet and prayed that his recovery would be smooth.

All of a sudden, Banks walked into the recovery room. He and Reid must have passed on the elevators.

Banks nodded to me.

I whispered that I was sorry.

The room was very quiet.

"I *was* furious with you," he said. "I dogged you out pretty good on the drive home. But then Thomas sat up and said, 'Daddy, don't be mad at Miss Dean. She took good care of me.' My heart melted. His voice was so tender and sincere."

I was overwhelmed at Banks's calm spirit. But I worried that I was experiencing the calm before the storm.

Later, when Thomas was settled in his room, Banks found Reid and me in the hallway. Banks put his arm around us and said, "I love you. It could just as easily have been *your* son, Jonathan, who got hurt while *I* was taking care of him. I'm a Christian. I can't let this accident ruin our friendship.

"I don't blame you," he continued. "It was a freak accident—one of those things. The world will see a difference in us by how we handle this."

I was relieved.

The Lord answered our prayers, and Thomas is now a healthy thirteen-year-old boy who was the starting shortstop for his Little League team last spring. And without a doubt Banks was right, the world has seen a difference in how this was handled.

> But the wisdom that comes from heaven is first of all pure; then peace-loving, considerate, submissive, full of mercy and good fruit, impartial and sincere.

Peacemakers who sow in peace raise a harvest of righteousness.

—James 3:17–18

Lord,

You are a compassionate and gracious God. You have granted Your strength to Your servants and given us a sign of Your goodness, that the world may see it and be drawn to put their hope in You.

Amen

Mother's Day Gift

BY CAROL GENENGELS

Kelly,* a young single mother, and her five-month-old son, Eric,* lived in public housing. She struggled to forget the mistakes of her past and make a new life for her and her little one. But she was determined to get off of public assistance and become self-sufficient as soon as possible.

Every Sunday she bundled up her baby and pushed him in his stroller to the little white church on the corner. She held Eric close, stroking his blonde curls as she sang hymns, prayed for guidance, and listened to sermons. God often spoke to Kelly through the pastor's messages.

Once a week Kelly carefully balanced her soiled laundry on the back of Eric's stroller and headed for the Laundromat. One afternoon as Kelly sorted dirty laundry into piles to take to the Laundromat, her friend Lisa* knocked on her door. She was in tears. "My children have nothing clean to wear and I'm flat broke. Can I please borrow enough money to do my laundry?"

Kelly knew if she gave money to Lisa, she wouldn't be able do her own laundry. Words from the pastor's Sunday sermon echoed in her mind. " *'Give, and it will be given to you. A good measure, pressed down, shaken together and running over, will be poured into your lap. For with the measure you use, it will be measured to you' (Luke 6:38). Remember, Jesus gave His all; He gave His very life! When you are asked to give, give as the Lord did. Give until it hurts!"*

> *"Do you know anybody who could use a washer and dryer?"*

Kelly reluctantly handed her laundry money to her friend and thought, *It hurts, Lord!*

Lisa thanked and hugged Kelly and went on her way.

Kelly scooped up her dirty clothes and tossed them back into the hamper. She sank into an armchair. In a few days it would be her first Mother's Day, a painful reminder that she had no husband or father for her baby.

Kelly had just put Eric down for his nap when the phone rang. It was the pastor of the church she attended. "Kelly, my wife and I were praying and we thought of you. Do you know anybody who could use a free washer and dryer?"

"I sure do!" Kelly said. "Me!"

"We just bought a brand new set—but the old ones work fine," the pastor said, "if you don't mind the color."

"Oh, Pastor, you don't know what this means to me!" Kelly went on to explain how his words had convicted her to "give until it hurts."

God, the husband to the husbandless and the father to the fatherless, had not forgotten her and Eric. He had multiplied her meager laundry money into something far more valuable—her own washer and dryer. The appliances were delivered to her apartment the day before Mother's Day. They are a constant reminder to Kelly of God's faithfulness to His beloved children.

> You will be made rich in every way so that you can be generous on every occasion, and through us your generosity will result in thanksgiving to God.
>
> —2 Corinthians 9:11

Lord,

My defense remains strong and steady for I rest in Your Strength that does not fail me. You are the One Who helps me. You are the Almighty, Who blesses me. Let Your blessings continue to rest upon my head.

Amen

God, Can
We
Talk?

By Jan Coates

One bright, sunny morning in Boston during the first week of April 1991, Matthew crawled into bed with me, put his arms around me, and propped his legs over mine. This was his way of ensuring that I didn't get up and that he had me as a captive audience.

Matthew, our adopted son, was almost four and his imagination and creativity had blossomed to the point where everything was a game. He put his little arms around me and said, "God called me on the telephone last night."

I laughed. I would have imagined Matthew saying he saved Lois Lane or visited a foreign planet before I would have ever thought that he would come up with the idea of a telephone call from God.

"Tell me," I asked, "what did God say?"

Matthew looked me right in the eye and said, "God told me that I have a baby."

As we went about preparing breakfast, I kept thinking about Matthew's prayers over the past several years. Every morning on the way to aerobics, the playground, or wherever we were going, we paused to say a prayer in the car. It was a way to regroup and calm our emotions. Getting Matthew out the door, even at age four, was always a challenge. He didn't want to go, and once he got to where we were going he didn't want to leave. Go figure.

Four-year-old Matthew said, "I got a telephone call from God last night."

Matthew's prayers in the car usually started out with a list of thank-you items to God and then progressed to his wish list. He always asked for a baby sister or brother—but he really wanted a sister.

It was hard for me to hear those prayers. For three years we had been on the "approved" list to adopt a second baby from a Christian adoption agency. As the years crept by, we began to think that a second child was not in God's plans.

Nevertheless, Bill, my husband, Matthew, and I prayed persistently with passion and faith that our heavenly Father would bless us with a second child.

About a week had passed since Matthew's "phone call from God," when our phone rang with a long-distance call from the adoption agency. The cheerful voice told us we had been selected by a birthmother to parent her newborn baby.

"Hallelujah! Praise the Lord!" I shouted. "Ring the bells, because a new life has entered His kingdom!"

The caller told us that our baby was healthy and that a few minor legal technicalities were pending.

When I shared the news with Matthew, he was not the least bit surprised. He boldly proclaimed, "Well, I told you so!"

Now I believed that Matthew had a direct line to God. While we were driving one day, I asked Matthew, "Did God tell you if the baby is a boy or girl?"

"No," Matthew said, "but I will ask Him."

I looked over at Matthew and smiled.

He furrowed his eyebrows and said, "Don't look at me while I call God on the phone, OK?"

So I looked straight ahead, driving, pretending not to notice the odd position my son had taken in the front seat. He curled up with his back facing me, his head tucked in toward his chest as he whispered with God.

Matthew, in his typical bold and unwavering faith in God, completed his "conversation," straightened his seat, and looked straight ahead out the front window of the car.

The suspense was driving me wild. "Well, what did God say?"

Matthew replied in his matter-of-fact manner, "Oh yeah, God said we have a baby girl."

The next week the adoption agency gave us the go-ahead to fly to the Midwest and see our new baby girl, Jordan Nicole Coates.

During the flight, Matthew witnessed to every person with which he came in contact. He shared his testimony, his phone calls to God, and his personal experiences with God. I think he planted more seeds for Christ on that one airplane ride than most people do in a lifetime. Perhaps that's why the Bible tells us to have the faith of a child!

Every one of God's children, regardless of age, can call on God. All we have to do, in Matthew's words, is "dial and smile."

> Therefore, whoever humbles himself like this child is the greatest in the kingdom of heaven.

> —Matthew 18:4

Lord,

I desire to pursue righteousness, faith, love and peace, and be counted along with those who call on You out of a pure heart.

Amen

$\mathcal{L}$ove $\mathcal{E}$xtravagantly

By Marita Littauer

My book *You've Got What It Takes!* includes a chapter about the value of a mission statement. While I was writing that chapter, I examined my life. I realized that I had a defining statement or theme for my professional ventures, but I did not have a personal one. I was recommending such statements to my readers, but I did not have one myself. I needed a personal purpose statement—a stated "path" for my personal life.

I had been attending a women's Bible study on the Book of Ephesians at my church. As a part of my preparation for each study, I read the chapter to be covered each week in several different versions of the Bible. The night before one class I read Ephesians 5 in

The Message. I wasn't looking for a personal mission statement, although it had been in the back of my mind.

As I read, a verse jumped out at me and I knew it was my personal "path"—at least for now. "Observe how Christ loved us. His love is not cautious but extravagant. He didn't love in order to get something from us but to give everything of Himself to us. Love like that" (Ephesians 5:2). I understood that my personal mission was to love my husband with extravagance, not to get but to give everything of myself. As I cooked breakfast or dinner, washed the dishes, and did the laundry, I could give, not expecting to get in return.

My husband, Chuck, was in the midst of a rough time. He was not able to give much right then.

But I was. I wrote that verse and placed it on my mirror in the bathroom to remind me that was my mission. I still frequently have to repeat this mission statement to myself as it is contrary to my human nature.

Shortly after taking on this idea of loving extravagantly, I was put to the test. Chuck has a large, radio-controlled, model airplane that has been a part of his life for over twenty years. He built it and has too much of himself invested in it to risk flying it.

With a five-foot wingspan, you cannot tuck it in some corner of the house or garage. It has traveled with us to eight different houses. In our current home it hangs up near the peak of the cathedral ceiling in the family room. It is bright red with Red Baron-like decals. You can't miss it. Since it is important to Chuck, I have accepted it as a conversation piece—and you can be sure it is!

Recently, he took the airplane to a model airplane show. Before the show he spent hours cleaning off the dust that had firmly attached itself to every surface. The plane was very popular at the show and he discovered how valuable it really is. Before he put it back on its hook, he wanted to protect it. So he covered the body and wings with plastic dry-cleaning bags—advertising and all.

When I saw it I wailed. "I'll never be able to entertain again! How do you expect me to have guests with those baggy dry-cleaning bags hanging up there!"

> *When I saw the plastic dry-cleaning bags, I wailed.*

I knew I was overreacting but I couldn't help myself. I like my home to look like a showplace. *I can't have advertising hanging up there. What an eyesore! The bags ought to have a warning to keep away from babies* and husbands!

I went outside and trimmed my roses, trying to cool off. As I took a deep breath, *"love extravagantly"* came to mind. *Does it really matter if the airplane has a bag over it? What is more important—that my husband be happy or that I have a lovely home?* Hmm. That was tough.

Love extravagantly, I told myself.

I went back inside and apologized—ready to accept the dry-cleaning bags.

Meanwhile, Chuck had decided that I was right. He had taken the plane down, removed the dry-cleaning bags, and was replacing them with clear plastic wrap that clings tightly to every curve and doesn't even show!

Ah, the power of a personal mission statement—not cautious but extravagant, not to get but to give. Love extravagantly.

> And now these three remain: faith, hope and love. But the greatest of these is love.
>
> —1 Corinthians 13:13

Lord,

**I choose to follow the way of love and I
eagerly desire spiritual gifts, especially the
gifts which strengthen, encourage and
comfort others.**

Amen

Ugly Cat

By Ava Chambers

A sickening groan pervaded my kitchen. Turning from the sink, I shook the water from my hands and walked toward the washing machine. An electrical burning smell cautioned me as I lifted the lid to find a pile of clothes soaking in suds. I feared the old machine had spun its last. Tears ran down my face, and I felt stupid. I shouldn't cry about a washing machine, but it seemed my whole year had been awful and it was only the end of March.

As I stood there wondering what to do, I heard the excited chatter of my children coming home from school. Thinking about my brood of four brought more tears. I just had to have a washing machine.

Sara, my ten year old, came into the room and instantly wrapped her arms around my waist. "What's the matter, Mama?" Her sweet voice was almost too much for me. She was the most sensitive of my children.

"I'm just being silly, Sara," I replied. "I think we're gonna have to find a way to buy a new washing machine."

"Is that all, Mama? Don't worry. Just ask God. Have faith."

> "*That cat must be the ugliest creature God ever made.*"

With that she bounded outside, leaving me alone with my doubts. All I had heard the past few weeks from the pulpit, in Sunday school, and now from my child was "Have faith and pray. Have faith and pray." I sat down at the kitchen table and put my head in my hands.

My worries were interrupted by the noise of discord. The children were fighting over the kitten again. We had adopted a stray, but I never imagined such a small cat could cause so much strife.

I sent the children inside and put the kitten in its box. *It must be the ugliest creature God ever made,* I thought. She looked like somebody had slung gold paint all over her black fur. Her eyes were a strange yellow color that haunted me.

The children liked her, though, and I had to admit she was affectionate. She purred so loudly we couldn't help but giggle.

Sara woke early the next day, Saturday, and went straight to the back door. As I lay in my bed I heard her calling the kitten. From the sound of her voice I could tell she was walking around to the front porch. I hoped she was dressed or had at least remembered her bedroom slippers. I waited for the sound of her coming back in. I was sure she would sneak the kitten in the house.

Instead, I heard tears.

Struggling out of bed, I started toward the kitchen.

Sara met me halfway. She fell into my arms, but she was crying so hard I couldn't understand what she said. I finally calmed her enough to discover the kitten was missing.

"Come across the road with me," she begged. "We must look in the woods."

> *I couldn't face the task of telling my children about another death.*

"Let's wait a little," I said. "It's early. She's probably sleeping in a new spot. We'll look after everyone gets up and gets dressed." I prayed the kitten would show up, but something inside me told me it was over—her kitten was gone forever.

A few hours later we began the search. It didn't take long for my husband and me to locate the kitten. She was in the woods and she was dead—apparently she'd been hit by a car and thrown several feet. We had suffered so much death in our family lately, my dad in January, my aunt in February, a great-aunt in March. I didn't want to see my children cry again. I asked my husband to tell the children while I cowardly stayed in the backyard.

After a while Sara came outside. I could tell she had been crying, but she looked happy as she came to me. I folded her deep in my arms, kissed the top of her head, and told her I was sorry about her kitten. She smiled up at me as if she had a secret.

Moving to sit beside me, Sara said, "Mama, can we go to the park and play?"

When I nodded she gave me a huge kiss.

As she stepped away from me I noticed a strange look on her face. "Sara, are you all right?" I asked.

"Yes, Mama," she replied. "My kitty is waiting for me at the park."

"Why do you think that? Didn't Daddy tell you what happened to her?" Concern filled my heart as I looked at a child that seemed to be unable or unwilling to face facts.

"Yes, Mama. Daddy told me, but I know there's a kitty at the park for me. I prayed and I told God that I really needed my kitty. You always told me that God answers our prayers, and my Sunday school teacher says all we need is faith."

I was sick of hearing people say, "Have faith"!

There was that "have faith" statement again. I was sick of hearing it. I couldn't let her go to the park expecting to find another kitten. It would hurt too much to be disappointed. "Let's make cookies," I said. "Or how about if I take you shopping?"

"No!" Sara shook her head. "We're supposed to go to the park and pick up the kitten."

Soon the other children chimed in. Apparently Sara had convinced her siblings about her message from God.

"All right," I said. We packed a snack and walked a few blocks to the park. With each step I felt as if I were heading to the gallows. My husband held my hand, each of us quiet with our own thoughts.

The children ran ahead. As they rounded the corner I heard Sara scream, "Maaa! Maaa!"

In an instant Sara ran back to us with a kitten tucked under her chin. It appeared to be the exact twin of the one that had been killed. She spun around with it, and then carried it up the steps of the playground slide and prepared for a ride down.

"Faith!" she yelled as she slid down.

The kitten is grown now and has her own brood of four kittens. At times I still feel overwhelmed, but then I look outside and see the ugliest cat in the world sitting on my doorstep. Then I remember the faith of a little girl and I am comforted.

> My message and my preaching were not with wise and persuasive words, but with a demonstration of the Spirit's power, so that your faith might not rest on men's wisdom, but on God's power.
>
> —1 Corinthians 2:4–5

Lord,

In this I greatly rejoice, though now for a little while we may have had to suffer grief, these have come so that our faith may be proved genuine and may result in praise when Jesus Christ is revealed.

Amen

Can I Preach without a Voice?

BY DR. JAMES L. WILSON

Slowly I surfaced to consciousness. Where was I? Lying in a strange room, hurting and struggling for breath, I tried to speak, but nothing came out. I lifted my right arm from the blanket and moved it around. Soon I felt the warmth of a stranger's hand.

"You're OK, Mr. Wilson. The surgery went great. Your wife is anxious to see you."

Thirty minutes later they rolled me back to my room. My wife, Susan, was there waiting.

"Was there any nerve damage?" I whispered. "What did the doctor say? Will my voice return?"

"The doctor doesn't know," she said. "He'll know more tomorrow."

Tomorrow came, and the first doctor I saw was the anesthesiologist. She asked how I was doing.

"I can't talk," I said in a raspy whisper.

"Do you mean it hurts to talk?"

"No," I croaked. "I *can't* talk."

She looked shocked and began to fumble with her chart, murmuring something about it maybe being temporary. Then she left the room without saying good-bye.

She knows something, I thought. *What happened in that operating room?*

That evening the surgeon appeared.

"Hi, doctor," I whispered.

He looked disappointed, but he sat on the bed and drew a diagram of what they had discovered during the surgery. A normal nerve to the vocal cord, he told me, is white and runs along the back of the thyroid gland. Mine was yellow and seemed to run through the middle. He tapped it to see if it was fatty tissue, but it would not break away. The assistant surgeon assured the doctor it was not the nerve and advised he cut it.

He asked for the instruments and got ready to sever the tissue—when something stopped him. He put the tools away, but the damage had been done. The tapping, he said, had frozen the nerve. "The function may return—or it may not," he concluded.

"But I'm a preacher," I said. "What do I do without a voice?"

The week before while working at my computer, I had sensed an unusual tightness in my neck. I went into the office bathroom and looked in the mirror. That's when I saw it above my collarbone—a lump.

I immediately thought of John Black, a parishioner of mine years ago. I could hear his raspy voice in my mind. Did I have cancer of the larynx like John? Would I lose my voice too? In those ten seconds, I discovered a lump, diagnosed my illness, resigned from my job, and visualized my funeral.

Two days later I visited my doctor. He reassured me I did not have cancer of the larynx. If it was cancer at all, it was in my thyroid. "If you have to have a cancer, that's the kind to have," he said. "It's the most curable."

What happened in the operating room?

He sent me to a hospital for an ultrasound. The procedure was quick and painless, so I went back to the office for a few minutes. It was Friday and I wanted to make sure everything was ready for Sunday morning. I opened my Bible and reviewed Sunday's sermon.

I had titled the message "When God Intervenes to Stop Us." In the sermon I looked at the story of God stopping King David from building the temple. The message—sometimes God stops us from doing something we want to do so that we'll do something He wants us to do. The sermon ended with a question for the congregation: "Do you want to know God's will, or do you want to *do* God's will?"

Now I lay nearly mute in a hospital bed, managing to whisper to the surgeon, "Will my voice come back?"

He looked away. "I don't know. Maybe."

Suddenly my theology and reality met face-to-face—and my theology blinked. Would I ever preach again? How would I earn a living? What about my family?

Back home that night I lay in bed, praying. *"God, I'm over here. Why are You doing this to me? Why don't You heal me?"*

The words from my last sermon came to mind. I felt God asking, *"Jim, do you want to know My will or do you want to do My will?"*

"God, I'm willing to do Your will, but please, let my voice return. That will really glorify You if You give me back my voice. You could do it during–"

In the middle of the sentence, I stopped short. *What if God doesn't heal me?*

Waiting wasn't hard at first. I had been told that normal function could return within two months. My church was willing to wait, and so was I.

> *In ten seconds at the mirror, I diagnosed my illness, resigned, and visualized my funeral.*

In the beginning, people's prayers touched me. One evening a six-year-old girl prayed, "Jesus, please give Preacher back his voice so we can listen to him preach again."

I lost it—tears trickled down my cheeks. I knew God would answer the prayers of this little angel.

But as the end of the two-month period neared, I began to resent the prayers as constant reminders that God wasn't doing anything to help me. I even chided our ministry staff for spending so much time praying for me.

My wife and my mother were my greatest encouragers. My mother was confident God would heal me. "He wouldn't call you to preach without supplying you a voice," she said.

"Sure, Mom," I retorted. "Just like he healed Lori." Lori—my little sister who had died less than a month before from lupus.

At church, attendance began to drop, people stopped joining, and giving fell below the budget. I continually prayed for my voice to return. But God did not put His words in my mouth.

I sat in silence and watched others preach in my pulpit for three months. Though I was grateful for their willingness to fill the pulpit, I resented their booming voices and became inwardly critical of their sermon content and delivery. Their presence in my pulpit was a constant reminder to me that I was no longer a preacher.

If I wasn't a preacher, who was I?

I underwent a second operation to move the paralyzed vocal cord over so it could touch the healthy one and produce sound. This surgery allowed me to speak slightly above a breathy whisper. It was an improvement, but we were hoping for so much more.

God forced me to sit in silence, listening while others filled my pulpit.

I returned to the pulpit. Preaching hurt physically, but worse than the physical pain, it was emotionally devastating. For the first time in my ministry, I saw people's eyes glaze over while I preached. I was forced to speak in a choppy, weak monotone, taking a breath every seven seconds. (The average person can speak for twenty-one seconds without taking a breath.)

Three months after the second operation, the doctor examined me. He recommended further surgery, this time from the Nashville specialist who had taught him the procedure. The last thing I wanted was another operation, but I was ready if I could get my voice back.

The third operation worked. Today I have a near-normal voice and can preach without help.

And, after two unsuccessful surgeries, I realize why we call doctors "practicing physicians." They are not perfect; they are still practicing.

Me? I'm still a "practicing preacher," not perfect, still learning as I go. I'm ashamed of some of my actions and attitudes. I'm not proud that I asked God: "Why are You doing this to me?" Yet I know the question is a statement of faith. It presupposes that God exists, and that He loves me and is in control of my destiny.

Things are different now. I listen more and talk less. I realize, too, that God's love for me is not dependent on what I do for Him. And every Sunday morning before I preach, I thank God for my voice.

> The grace of our Lord was poured out on me abundantly, along with the faith and love that are in Christ Jesus. Here is a trustworthy saying that deserves full acceptance: Christ Jesus came into the world to save sinners—of whom I am the worst. But for that very reason I was shown mercy so that in me, the worst of sinners, Christ Jesus might display his unlimited patience as an example for those who would believe on him and receive eternal life.
>
> —1 Timothy 1:14–16

Lord,

I rejoice in Your strength. How great is my joy in the victories You give! You have granted me the desire of my heart and have not withheld the request of my lips.

Amen

Among Us

BY DANA LYNN POPE

It was a warm, sunny day in March when I toured the Pater Noster near Jerusalem. Many believed this small cave to be the spot where Jesus taught the disciples how to pray. Jesus was available centuries ago to the disciples in much the same way as the Holy Spirit is available to us today. At least that is what I had been told.

I thought the disciples were luckier since they had been in the cave with Jesus, and I was only seeing it as part of a tour group.

I walked down the wide stone steps into the cave. Even though the cave was small, about the size of a two-car garage, it did not feel closed in. The large stones making up the walls to the cavern were cut smooth and stacked neatly on one another. These stones reflected the artificial light that was now installed in the corners.

During Jesus' time flickering fires built in the cave would have cast golden shadows on the walls.

Standing in the open room, I said the words our Lord taught his disciples, "Our Father, Who art in heaven. . . ." I tried to imagine what the disciples experienced when they heard these words spoken here.

I walked out the back door and climbed the stone stairs up to the church that is now perched on top of the cave. In Israel, any place of importance has a church built on it. In this case, a Crusader church was built over the Pater Noster.

I entered an arched breezeway to see walls filled with beautiful tiles. Each set contained the Lord's Prayer written in a different language. Each translation was five feet high, three feet across, and bordered by beautiful flowered tiles. Every language from English and French to Thai and Coreen was represented.

As I walked toward the doorway I could hear a group of Japanese tourists inside singing the Lord's Prayer in their native tongue. As the group I was with stepped inside the church, the Japanese tourists started to sing in English and we joined in.

An amazing thing happened while I stood there singing the Lord's Prayer. I felt an overwhelming sense of a force with me, something that encompassed the entire building and the sixty people in it. I trembled from the energy of this presence. My legs grew weak and my body shook. It was the most pleasant feeling, but it was also overpowering. The presence felt familiar, and I wanted to enjoy it, to soak it in. I knew without a doubt that it was the presence of the Holy Spirit among us.

Tears ran down my cheeks. I looked around the room and noticed that everyone had tears streaming down their faces, even the men. As the song ended everyone began hugging, and I knew each person in that room felt the same thing I felt. I understood Jesus' words in Matthew 18:20, "For where two or three come together in my name, there I am with them." And I knew the Holy Spirit exists to interact with us.

Aim for perfection, listen to my appeal, be of one mind, live in peace. And the God of love and peace will be with you.

—2 Corinthians 13:11

Lord,

Our Father which art in heaven, hallowed be thy name. Thy kingdom come. . . . For thine is the kingdom, and the power, and the glory, for ever.

Amen

A Final Call

to

*W*orship

BY BISHOP T. D. JAKES

P aul closes his prayer for the Ephesians with praise to God:

> Now unto him that is able to do exceeding abundantly above all that we ask or think, according to the power that worketh in us, Unto him be glory in the church by Christ Jesus throughout all ages, world without end. Amen. (Ephesians 3:20–21 KJV)

"Now unto Him." "Him" refers to our God, who loves us infinitely and is omnipotent with all might and strength. Paul says that He is "able to do exceeding abundantly above all that we ask or think," and the Greek language here indicates that the ability of our God transcends and goes far beyond the highest measure we could imagine. This is one of those phrases in Scripture where we intensely search for some English word that might even come close to portraying the fullness of God's power. In the end, the translators of the King James Version settled for "exceeding abundantly."

God wants us to know that He is *able*. No matter what we face in life, He is able to handle it—and He is able to empower us to handle it. Now we all know that it is nice to have someone who loves us, but if they aren't able, it's a bad situation! If God only loved us and didn't have power, we might be encouraged, but we would fail. On the other hand, if God only had power and didn't love us, we might be delivered, but we would feel crushed in our spirits. Thank God that is not the reality here! With both love and strength of God together, we have an unbeatable combination.

The might of the Spirit is beyond our comprehension. None of us can fathom the power of God in creating this entire universe and upholding it moment to moment. The love of Christ is beyond our knowing. None of us can ever fully fathom why God loves us, how much God loves us, or the countless manifestations of God's love toward us. Put them together—might and love—and there simply is no way we can take in all that truth and ecstasy! So how do we experience the full expression of God's might and love? Paul says this vast resource of God's love and might is experienced by us "according to the power that worketh in us" (Ephesians 3:20).

Here we have that word "according" again! In the first two chapters of Ephesians, "according" always referred to something God did. But in this verse in chapter 3, Paul is telling us that the degree to which we experience God and the success we achieve as Christians depends on the degree to which *we allow* the Spirit of God to fill us, empower us, illuminate us, and move us. And the way we allow the Spirit of God to transform us in this manner is to be a worshiper of God, to be completely His.

When we worship God, we open the floodgates of God's love and might toward us. We begin to understand the unsearchable riches of the wealth He has given us in Christ Jesus. We begin to understand how to walk the walk He has placed before us. We start knowing things that are unknowable, doing things that are not doable, having things that are not have-able, reaching things that are untouchable—according to His power that worketh in us. We can *know* He is able and loves us exceeding abundantly, beyond our imagination and reason, as we allow His Spirit free reign in our hearts and minds.

> *Worship allows the Spirit of God to fill us, empower us, illuminate us, and move us.*

Paul wrote to Timothy that God had not given us the spirit of fear—He did not give us a spirit of doubt, low self-esteem, or weakness—but rather, *love* and *power* and a *sound mind*. (See 2 Timothy 1:7.) He gave us His love, His power, and His wisdom. How? By the Holy Spirit. When Jesus was just about to return to heaven, He told His disciples not to go anywhere or do anything until they had received the power of the Holy Spirit. "And, behold, I send the promise of my Father upon you: but tarry ye in the city of Jerusalem, until ye be endued with power from on high" (Luke 24:49).

Read Luke's account of this in the Book of Acts 1:1–9. Of the hundreds of disciples who heard and saw Jesus at this time, only 120 remained to receive the power of the Holy Spirit in the upper room in Jerusalem, but what a time those 120 saints had! On the Day of Pentecost, they also experienced the fullness of the power that had calmed the stormy seas, cast a legion of demons from a raging man, and raised Lazarus from the dead.

When Jesus, true to His Word, poured out the Holy Ghost all over them, a mighty, rushing wind swept through the upper room, tongues of fire appeared on their heads, and fiery tongues of every kindred and tribe came gushing out of their innermost being. They hit the streets and Peter, who days before had denied the Lord three times and proved himself to be a base coward, preached a passionate, religion-busting, tradition-breaking, Holy Ghost message. In one day the same power that resurrected Jesus from the dead swept through the streets of Jerusalem and brought three thousand people into the kingdom of God! (See Acts 2.)

This is what God wants us to be walking in right now, this power to witness boldly and bring in a mighty harvest of souls, but it is "according to the power that worketh in us." According to . . . According to . . . We must have the power of the Holy Spirit operating full force and without hindrance in our lives to fulfill the mandate God has given us in these last days.

> For this cause I bow my knees unto the Father of our Lord Jesus Christ, of whom the whole family in heaven and earth is named.
>
> —Ephesians 3:14–15

Lord,

You did not send a spirit that makes me a slave again to fear, but when I received the Holy Spirit, I received the Spirit of sonship, and by Him I cry, "Abba, Father."

Amen

Scriptural Index for Prayers

Prayers throughout the book are taken from the following Scriptures, listed in the order they appear:

Credits

"May I Have the Pleasure?" by Beth Moore, taken from *A Heart Like His: Seeking the Heart of God through a Study of David,* video 6 of series (Nashville, TN: LifeWay, 2000). Used with permission. All rights reserved.

"Warning, Plane Problems!" by Jesse Duplantis, reprinted from *Jambalaya for the Soul* (Tulsa, OK: Harrison House, 2000). Used by permission. All rights reserved.

"Chopped Fruit" by Joyce Meyer, reprinted from *Help Me I'm Married!* (Tulsa, OK: Harrison House, 2000), 87–89. All rights reserved. Used by permission.

"The Power in Praise" by Merlin R. Carothers, reprinted from *Power in Praise* (Plainfield, NJ: Logos International, 1972). Used by permission. All rights reserved.

"The California Earthquake" by Billye Brim, adapted from *The Blood and the Glory* (Tulsa, OK: Harrison House, 1995). All rights reserved. Used by permission.

"Shaken Awake to Pray" by Oral Roberts, retold in third person from *A Prayer Cover over Your Life* (Tulsa, OK: Oral Roberts Ministry), 9–12. Used by permission.

"When Jesus Visited Our House" by T. L. Osborn, reprinted from *Healing the Sick*, 37ed. (Tulsa, OK: Harrison House, 1986). All rights reserved. Used by permission.

Contributors

Niki Anderson writes to share truths that are vital in her own life. She is author of the best-selling book *What My Cat Has Taught Me about Life*. Email: Nander1405@aol.com.

Karen Bean served as director of outreach and missions for a large church, has lived on the mission field, and leads teams. She and her husband train and encourage national ministers through their ministry, Nation to Nation. Email:gkbeanntn@aol.com.

Tamara Boggs is the author of *Children Are a Blessing from the Lord: Learning God's Wisdom through Our Children*. She resides in a centennial Midwestern farmhouse with her husband, three children, five cats, and two dogs. Email: taboggs@netdirect.net.

Cristine Bolley served as a development editor for major ministries including T. D. Jakes and Joyce Meyer. She is the author of *A Gift from St. Nicholas,* and coauthor of *When Every Hour's a Rush Hour* and *What I Learned from God while Quilting*. Cris is sole proprietor of Wings Unlimited, an editorial acquisition service. Email: WingsUnlimited2@aol.com.

Michael S. Bolley is the business manager for a law firm in Wichita, Kansas. He is also a freelance consultant, writer, musician, and Civil War reenactor. Email: Mike1025@aol.com.

Billye Brim is a frequent conference speaker and ministers in churches, Bible schools, family camps, and on television. The emphasis of her ministry is on the glory of God and His glorious church. Contact: P.O. Box 126, Collinsville, Oklahoma 74021.

Sue Ann Brown serves as the Minister of Music for Manger Baptist Church and as the Director of Public Information for Tulsa Community College, both in Tulsa, Oklahoma. She has been writing and publishing for more than twenty-five years. Email: sbrown3@tulsa.cc.ok.us.

Dr. James R. Burke is an ordained minister, ventriloquist, juggler, and Christian illusionist. He regularly performs in school assemblies, emphasizing character development. He is the pastor of Sandia Baptist Church, at 1100 W. Manana, Clovis, New Mexico 88101. Email: son-gazer@3lefties.com.

John Calhoun is a professional writer and amateur outdoors man. He has backpacked and skied all over the western United States, frequently publishing articles about these trips. He has been in deserts, in mountains, in swamps, and in trouble. Email: jcalhoun@frii.com.

Merlin R. Carothers served in the 82nd Airborne Division during World War 2 in France, Germany, and Belgium as a demolition expert. A master parachutist and civil air pilot, he now counsels and lectures extensively. He is the author of several books including *Power in Praise,* which may be purchased at local bookstores.

Ava Chambers is the mother of four children. Their constant questions and playful antics often grant her special insights. Ava prays that by sharing these stories they may touch a heart. Email: Acham922@aol.com.

Kitty Chappell is a freelance writer and speaker for Stonecroft Ministries Christian Women's Clubs and After Five Business and Professional Women's groups. She resides in Arizona. Email: KittChap@aol.com.

A. Starr Clay is a consultant, writer, and president of W. B. Freeman Concepts, Inc. She has coauthored or compiled over fifty-five books primarily in the Christian genre. Email: Astarr@aol.com.

Jan Coates is the married mother of two adopted children. She uses her experiences and personal relationship with the Lord to present keynote and workshop messages that offer encouragement and hope. Email: jmc1031@TCA.net.

Edwin Louis Cole is the founder of the Christian Men's Network, an organization dedicated to providing resources for creating men of integrity. Contact: www.edcole.org.

Bishop William Cox is the chaplain to Episcopal World Missions. A former lieutenant colonel in the army, Bishop Cox also served the Episcopal Church in Maryland for thirty years and was Assistant Bishop of Oklahoma and later of Texas. He and his wife conduct international teaching and healing conferences and reside in Tulsa, Oklahoma.

Victoria Craig was raised in Texas as a pastor's daughter. Her father is one of the top ten theologians according to *Who's Who in America*. Often feeling inadequate in the shadow of her father, Victoria found comfort in knowing God is no respecter of persons. Email: victoria.craig@ci.okc.ok.us.

Dean Crowe is a frequent speaker at women's events and a Bible study teacher. She is the married mother of two teenage boys. She has written an in-depth Bible study, *Qualities of a Wise Woman,* and can be reached at DeanRCrowe@aol.com.

Bruce A. Davis Sr. works full time as operations manager in a plumbing and heating company in Washington State. Bruce teaches and speaks to youth groups and men's groups about relationship and family issues. Email: badavis@nwlink.com.

Joy DeKok is the coauthor (with Cristine Bolley) of *Under His Wings* (Barbour Publishing). Joy enjoys watching birds, long walks with her husband, Jon, reading, and writing. Email: jdekok@aol.com.

Jesse Duplantis was saved and delivered from a life of addiction in 1974. Founder of Jesse Duplantis Ministries, Jesse spent more than twenty years as an evangelist. He delivers anointed teaching and humorous messages through his television program, which reaches millions worldwide. Website: www.jdm.org.

Mike Evans is an award-winning journalist, producer, and minister. The prime-time television specials he has hosted have received thirteen national awards. Contact: P.O. Box 910, Euless, Texas 76039–0910.

Eva Marie Everson is the author of several books, including *Shadow of Dreams*, *True Love: Engaging Stories of Real Life Proposals*, and *One True Vow*. A noted speaker, she also teaches Old Testament theology at Life Training Center in Orlando, Florida. Email: PenNhnd@aol.com.

Susan Gammon resides in a rural Kansas community with her husband and two teenage children. She enjoys sharing the love of Jesus with others through a music ministry at Worden United Methodist Church. Email: gammon@sound.net.

Carol Genengels is cofounder of a Woman's Touch Ministry. A wife and grandmother, Carol has a heart for intercession, speaking, and songwriting. Email:awtcarolg@aol.com.

Ben Groenewold, former co-owner of Southport Exploration, is a retired geologist who has traveled worldwide. A licensed lay preacher and lay eucharistic assistant with the Episcopal Church, he also has been a Stephen's minister and active in the Cursillo movement.

Sharon Hanby-Robie is the vice president of marketing at Starburst Publishers, a speaker, television personality, and the author of *My Name Isn't Martha But I Can Decorate My Home* series of books. Email: sharonrobie@starburstpublishers.com.

Karen Hardin and her husband are missionaries and have lived and worked in China for over ten years. They have three children. Email:kkhardin@gorilla.net.

Armené Humber is a freelance writer whose work has appeared in numerous publications. She is a career counselor and instructor with the Women's Opportunities Center at University of California, Irvine Extension. She can be reached at 714-775-6705 or armhumber@aol.com.

Bishop T. D. Jakes is the author of several books, including the best-sellers *Daddy Loves His Girls, Lay Aside the Weight, Loose That Man and Let Him Go!* and *Woman, Thou Art Loosed!* He is the founder and pastor of Potter's House Church in Dallas, one of the fastest-growing churches in the nation. Contact: T. D. Jakes Ministries, P.O. Box 210887, Dallas, Texas 75211.

Louise Tucker Jones is the author of the inspirational novel, *Dance from the Heart* and coauthor of the Gold Medallion Award–winning book, *Extraordinary Kids*. She is a popular speaker and has appeared on several radio and TV programs. Email: LouiseTJ@aol.com.

Charles Joulwan has been a prison chaplain for twenty-six years. Author of twenty tracts, which have been distributed to millions worldwide, Charlie has also trained twenty-five people to duplicate his ministry in their areas. Contact: P.O. Box 366, Elkton, Maryland 21922.

Laurie Klein approaches writing like dinner: hungry, curious, always wanting more. With interests in art, music, and theater, she exhibits, teaches, and performs in the Pacific Northwest and abroad. Email: ljbklein@yahoo.com.

Paige M. Kolb is a speaker and writer based in Atlanta, Georgia. As a former employee at CNN, she urges her audiences to hold the media accountable and to invest in future generations. Email: paigebr@aol.com.

Annetta P. Lee is the married mother of one daughter and three grandchildren. She and her husband, Kenneth, attend Northwest Christian Center in Oklahoma City. Email: aplee@ilinkusa.net.

Marita Littauer is a professional speaker and author of ten books, including *Personality Puzzle*, *Talking So People Will Listen*, and *Love Extravagantly*. Marita is the President of CLASServices, Inc., an organization that provides resources, training, and promotion for speakers and authors. Contact www.classervices.com or 800-433-6633.

Bishop Eddie Long is the senior pastor of New Birth Missionary Baptist Church in Atlanta, Georgia.

Vonda Mailen is the ministry director of Peace Officer and First Responder Prayer Partners International, an organization committed to pray for police, firefighters, and other authorities.

Contact www.perfectpresence.com/popp-pray; vmailen@sun-flower.com.

Robin Marsh is an Emmy nominated and national award-winning journalist who is currently anchor/reporter for KWTV NEWS 9 in Oklahoma City and a frequent speaker for Christian Women's Club. Email: marsh@kwtv.com.

Therese Marszalek is a wife and mother of three children. Therese is the author of *Breaking Out: A "for real" Look at the Process of Being Transformed into the Image of Jesus Christ* (forthcoming). Email: kingskids5@cfaith.com.

Tedi E. Martin has been involved with Lifeway Christian Resources in Nashville, Tennessee, for twenty-three years. She is the married grandmother of six and the prayer leader of her church choir. Email: tmartin@lifeway.com.

John Mason is a speaker and national best-selling author of *An Enemy Called Average* and founder of Insight International. Contact: Insight International, 8801 South Yale, Suite 410, Tulsa, OK 74137. Email: insight@ionet.net.

Joyce Meyer has been teaching the Word of God since 1976 and in full-time ministry since 1980. Joyce's *Life in the Word* radio and television programs are heard or seen internationally. She writes and travels extensively, conducting Life in the Word conferences. Contact: Joyce Meyer Ministries, P.O. Box 655, Fenton, Missouri 63026.

Beth Moore believes that her calling is Bible literacy: guiding believers to love and live God's Word. Beth loves the Lord, loves to laugh, and loves to be with His people. Contact: Living Proof Inc., 5870 Highway 6 North, Houston, Texas 77084.

Lynn D. Morrissey is founder of Noteworthy Living, Inc., editor of best-selling *Seasons of a Woman's Heart* and *Treasures of a Woman's Heart* (Starburst), contributing author to numerous best-selling devotionals, and CLASS speaker/staff member who specializes in prayer-journaling and woman's topics. Email: words@brick.net.

Cecil Murphey has written his eightieth book, *Seeking God's Hidden Face: When God Seems Absent* (InterVarsity Press). He has ghostwritten autobiographies for well-known personalities, including Franklin Graham, B. J. Thomas, Dino Karsanakas, and the million-copies-sold *Gifted Hands: The Ben Carson Story.* Email: Cec_Haraka@msn.com.

A. Koshy Muthalaly, Ph.D. is an ordained Baptist minister and former theological educator. Currently he teaches at the Southern Nazarene University, in Bethany, Oklahoma, in the Department of Adult Studies. Email: koshy@snu.edu.

Jessica Nichols is a praise and worship leader at Christ Community Church, as well as a teacher of Worship Workshop 101. The married mother of two grown children, she resides in Alamogordo, New Mexico. Email: jnichols@zianet.com.

Mary Marcia Lee Norwood is a former teacher and coach who writes and travels as a professional storyteller and speaker. She watches God's presence change the ordinary into extraordinary adventures in Missouri—as well as adventures in Israel, Egypt, China, and soon Russia. Email: mmln@unicom.net.

Ruth Woodbury-Craig Offutt continues a ministry of love through encouraging stories about her eighty-plus years of faith walks, which go to hundreds of people in the United States by mail and through her website (www.sunflower.com/~popppray/).

Dr. Lloyd Ogilvie is the sixty-first chaplain to the United States Senate. Prior to that appointment, he was pastor of the First Presbyterian Church of Hollywood, with a national radio and television ministry. He has authored over forty books, including *Asking God Your Hardest Questions.*

T. L. Osborn impacts the world as a minister and evangelist. He and his wife have probably led more people to Jesus Christ in non-Christian lands, and may have witnessed more great healing miracles than any other couple who has ever yet lived. Contact: OSFO, Box 10, Tulsa, Oklahoma 74102.

Dana Lynn Pope speaks on topics relating to spiritual habits. As a wife and mother of two, she along with five other families started St. Nicholas Church in Flower Mound. Dana serves there as director of programs, in teaching discipleship, and on committees. Email: Popedana@aol.com.

Rev. Anna P. Rich, D.D. pastors a church in rural Fort Mojave, Arizona. She is a speaker, author, and poet who gives seminars on social issues from a biblical perspective. Email: Drannette@ctaz.com.

Oral Roberts is the founder and chancellor of Oral Roberts University in Tulsa, Oklahoma. An internationally acclaimed evangelist, he is also regarded as a pioneer in Christian broadcasting and is the author of more than 120 books. He is also the founding chairman of International Charismatic Bible Ministries. Contact: Oral Roberts Evangelistic Association, P.O. Box 2187, Tulsa, Oklahoma 74102-2187.

Richard Roberts is the president and chief executive officer of Oral Roberts University. He and his wife, Lindsay, host a nationally syndicated daily television program, *Something Good Tonight: The Hour of Healing*. Richard has conducted healing crusades on six continents. Contact: Oral Roberts Evangelistic Association, P.O. Box 2187, Tulsa, Oklahoma 74102-2187.

Suzy Ryan is a mother of three and a freelance writer living in California. Email: kensuzyr@aol.com.

Carol Sallee is a speaker, author, pastor's wife, and the mother of three teenagers. She is the founder of To Know Christ Ministries. Email: carolsallee@yahoo.com. Visit www.carolsallee.com.

Troy Sledge has been involved in short-term missions work since 1984. He teaches the missions course for nursing students at Oral Roberts University. Email: sledgers@aol.com.

Rev. Stan Tate D. Min., a former smokejumper, is chaplain to Idaho Smokejumpers. He earns his living as a bioethicist for hospitals and health organizations. He is author of *Jumping Skyward: Wilderness Spirituality*. Email: stantate@turbonet.com.

Nanette Thorsen-Snipes has written more than 400 articles, columns, devotions, and books for such publications and publishing companies as *Breakaway*, *HomeLife*, Honor Books, and Multnomah Publishers. Contact: P.O. Box 1596, Buford, GA 30515. Email: nsnipes@mindspring.com. Website: www. nanettesnipes.com.

Becky Weber is a freelance writer and founder of Fragrance Ministries. She resides in Couer d'Alene, Idaho. Becky is a national speaker at churches, conferences, and women's retreats. Email: fragranceministries@yahoo.com.

Michael R. Wells is deeply indebted to all of those who have shared their lives in Christ with him and helped him to grow.

Elizabeth Wietholter served as a Christian counselor in Tulsa for ten years and now works full time in writing and curriculum development. She is the author of *Victorious Worshipers of God from Age 3*. Email: eaglemount@bigfoot.com.

Dr. James L. Wilson is the pastor of Lighthouse Baptist Church in Seaside, California, and the online editor at www.Fresh-Ministry.org. Contact: Lighthouse Baptist Church 1030 Hilby Ave., Seaside, CA 93955 Email:jwilson@freshministry.org.

Margolyn Woods, a former Rose Bowl Queen and actress, lives in Oklahoma with her husband and three of their five children. She is the author of seven books and a popular speaker for women's events and conferences across the country. Email: Margolyn@mmcable.com.

JoAnn R. Wray, a writer, editor, and artist since 1974, is Director of Publications for Fellowship of Christian Writers. In February 2001, she launched Melody of the Heart E-zine at http://epistle-works.com/HeartMelody. Email: epistle@epistleworks.com.

Michael E. Wray is a network administrator with Family Connect. On scholarship following a life-threatening battle with cancer, Michael is editor of the Friends University paper. Email: mwray@epistleworks.com.

POPULAR BOOKS BY STARBURST PUBLISHERS®

Stories for the Spirit-Filled™ Believer
Edited by Cristine Bolley
It's one thing to know that God is real. It is quite another to have profound and on-going experiences that confirm that belief. In this awesome collection of stories, Cristine Bolley compiles the real-life testimonies of believers who have heard God's voice and responded. This volume includes stories from today's most dynamic Charismatic personalities: Oral Roberts, Jesse Duplantis, T. D. Jakes, Joyce Meyer, and more. Each selection contains a Scripture verse, true story, and a prayer. Sure to inspire readers to listen for God's voice in their own lives.
(trade paper) ISBN 1892016540 **$13.99**

Bible Seeds: A Simple Study-Devotional for Growing in God's Word
From the Creators of the God's Word for the Biblically-Inept™ *series*
Growing your faith is like tending a garden—just plant the seed of God's Word in your heart, tend it with prayer, and watch it blossom. At the heart of this unique study is a Bible verse or "seed" that is combined with an inspirational lesson, a word study, application tips, thought questions with room to write, a prayer starter, and a final thought.
(trade paper) ISBN 1892016443 **$13.99**

An Expressive Heart: Stories, Lessons, and Exercises Inspired by the Psalms
Edited by Kathy Collard Miller
An intimate book of inspirational lessons from the best-selling editor of the *God's Abundance* collection. Each selection includes a passage from the poetic Book of Psalms, an inspirational story, lesson, quotation, and idea for personal journaling with room to write. The Psalms provide an unmatched guide for anyone who wants to know God better, and *An Expressive Heart* will help you say what's on your heart.
(trade paper) ISBN 1892016508 **$12.99**

A Growing Heart: Stories, Lessons, and Exercises Inspired by Proverbs
Edited by Kathy Collard Miller
The profound truths of Proverbs provide wisdom for making good

choices in life. Each selection includes a verse from Proverbs, an inspirational story, teachings, quotation, and idea for journaling with room to write. Lessons will guide the reader on topics such as discipline, friendship, love, parenting, wealth, and work.
(trade paper) ISBN 1892016524 **$12.99**

The God Things Come in Small Packages series will make you want to blow the dust off your rose-colored glasses, open your eyes, and recount God's blessings! Join best-selling writers LeAnn Weiss, Susan Duke, Caron Loveless, and Judith Carden as they awaken your senses and open your mind to the "little" wonders of God in life's big picture!

God Things Come in Small Packages:
Celebrating the Little Things in Life
(hard cover) ISBN 1892016281 **$12.95**

God Things Come in Small Packages for Moms:
Rejoicing in the Simple Pleasures of Motherhood
(hard cover) ISBN 189201629X **$12.95**

God Things Come in Small Packages for Friends:
Exploring the Freedom of Friendship
(hard cover) ISBN 1892016346 **$12.95**

God Things Come in Small Packages for Women:
Celebrating the Unique Gifts of Women
(hard cover) ISBN 1892016354 **$12.95**

The Bible—God's Word for the Biblically-Inept™
By Larry Richards
An excellent book to start learning the entire Bible. Get the basics or the in-depth information you are seeking with this user-friendly overview. From Creation to Christ to the Millennium, learning the Bible has never been easier.
(trade paper) ISBN 0914984551 **$16.95**

Revelation—God's Word for the Biblically-Inept™
By Daymond R. Duck
End-time Bible Prophecy expert Daymond R. Duck leads us verse by verse through one of the Bible's most confusing books. Follow the experts as they

forge their way through the captivating prophecies of Revelation!
(trade paper) ISBN 0914984985 **$16.95**

John—God's Word for the Biblically-Inept™
By Lin Johnson
From village fisherman to beloved apostle, John was an eyewitness to the teachings and miracles of Christ. Now, readers can join in an easy-to-understand, verse-by-verse journey through the fourth and most unique of all the Gospels. Witness the wonder of Jesus, a man who turned water into wine, healed the blind, walked on water, and raised Lazarus from the dead.
(trade paper) ISBN 1892016435 **$16.95**

Mark—God's Word for the Biblically-Inept™
By Scott Pinzon
The shortest of all the Gospels, Mark focuses on Jesus' actions. Telling the story of the adult Jesus from the time of his baptism by John the Baptist to his crucifixion and resurrection, readers will learn about the Book of Mark in simple, vivid terms that will bring it to life like never before!
(trade paper) ISBN 1892016362 **$17.99**

Life of Christ, Volume 1—God's Word for the Biblically-Inept™
By Robert C. Girard
Take a journey through the Gospels of Matthew, Mark, Luke, and John, tracing the story of Jesus from his virgin birth to his revolutionary ministry. Icons, illustrations, and features help readers learn about Jesus' baptism, Sermon on the Mount, miracles, and parables.
(trade paper) ISBN 1892016230 **$16.95**

Life of Christ, Volume 2—God's Word for the Biblically-Inept™
By Robert C. Girard
Life of Christ, Volume 2, begins with events recorded in Matthew 16, where volume 1 ends. Read about Jesus' transfiguration, triumphal ride through Jerusalem, capture in the Garden of Gethsemane, and his trial, crucifixion, resurrection, and ascension. Find out how to be great in the kingdom of God, what Jesus meant when he called himself the light of the world, and what makes up real worship.
(trade paper) ISBN 1892016397 **$16.95**

• **Learn more at www.biblicallyinept.com** •

Purchasing Information
www.starburstpublishers.com

Books are available from your favorite bookstore, either from current stock or special order. To assist bookstores in locating your selection, be sure to give title, author, and ISBN. If unable to purchase from a bookstore, you may order direct from STARBURST PUBLISHERS. When ordering please enclose full payment plus shipping and handling as follows:

Post Office (4th class)
$4.00 with purchase of up to $20.00
$5.00 ($20.01–$50.00)
9% of purchase price for purchases of $50.01 and up

Canada
$5.00 (up to $35.00)
15% ($35.01 and up)

United Parcel Service (UPS)
$5.00 (up to $20.00)
$7.00 ($20.01–$50.00)
12% ($50.01 and up)

Overseas
$5.00 (up to $25.00)
20% ($25.01 and up)

Payment in U.S. funds only. Please allow two to four weeks minimum for delivery by USPS (longer for overseas and Canada). Allow two to seven working days for delivery by UPS. Make checks payable to and mail to:

Starburst Publishers®
P.O. Box 4123
Lancaster, PA 17604

Credit card orders may be placed by calling 1-800-441-1456, Mon.–Fri., 8:30 A.M. to 5:30 P.M. Eastern Standard Time. Prices are subject to change without notice. Catalogs are available for a 9 x 12 self-addressed envelope with four first-class stamps.

Understanding the Bible Is Just a Click Away!

Starburst Publishers brings you the best internet sites for
homeschool, Sunday School, individual, group, and teen Bible study!

www.biblicallyinept.com

View our FREE weekly Bible study on-line or have
it delivered to your e-mail address at no charge!
It's the *What the Bible Says about . . .*™ weekly Bible study
from Dr. Larry Richards, General Editor of the
best-selling *God's Word for the Biblically-Inept*™ series.

---

www.homeschoolteach.com
www.sundayschoolteach.com

Each of these two sites offers a FREE e-newsletter with resources, fresh ideas,
activities, news updates, and more! You will also find the internet's first
downloadable homeschool and Sunday School Bible curriculums!

www.learntheword.com

NEW—Just for TEENS! Sign up for a FREE weekly Bible study or
have it delivered to your e-mail address at no charge! You will
also find information about books for getting close to God!

The Bible Made Easy!